It's a
Playboy
World

It's a Playboy World

William S. Banowsky

FLEMING H. REVELL COMPANY
OLD TAPPAN, NEW JERSEY

To my mother,

who made our home a happy place,
and who inspired us to believe
there is something beyond
mere happiness.

Contents

Foreword

WHAT IS NEEDED in our widespread moral confusion, is not moral philosophy in general, however valuable that may have been in the past, but a particularized handling of contemporary live options. There is little doubt that the single most popular philosophy in America today is not a system espoused in some university, but that which has been popularized by the name "playboy." There is, of course, nothing really new about this special complex of ideas. It is but a modern revival of the ancient doctrine of Hedonism. Hedonism is the philosophy which holds that the pursuit of pleasure is life's highest purpose. What is new in our time, however, is the very widespread acceptance of this position as a way of life. There is much evidence that the conventional American middle-class is drifting toward a life style which is clearly hedonistic.

This book is one man's effort to take the implications of the popular philosophy seriously. In his analysis of the playboy cult, Dr. Banowsky is not concerned with the influence of a magazine or with any specific personality, but with a life philosophy; and the philosophy which he examines is far more pervasive than many of us may wish to admit. It is true that Mr. Hugh M. Hefner has perhaps most cogently reduced the current practice to a creed, *The Playboy Philosophy;* and everybody knows that the magazine which he edits has done much to promote the modern cult. But this book deals, not with Hugh Hefner, but with the moral crisis of our time. The important thing about Hefner is not what he is causing but what he is reflecting about the mood of our society. His magazine, one of the most widely read journals on American college campus, serves to symbolize the general appeal of the pleasure cult.

The present preoccupation with the pursuit of pleasure is not limited, by any means, to those who have read the official publications of the movement. The widespread idea, regularly expressed in clubs, on airplanes and in college dormitories, is that we have been liberated from old and restrictive taboos and set free to do what we please. Even those who have done little reading express approval by saying that at last we have something which takes away all debilitating feelings of guilt. It is now possible, they say, to be ourselves, and to express our desires, whatever they may be, without the burden of conscience. The attitude is one of absolute freedom and everyone can "do his own thing." This revised version of an old gospel is no frivolous matter, but a highly articulate and imposing moral philosophy which has tremendous influence in our society.

Dr. Banowsky did not seek to be involved with the playboy creed, but was initially drawn into an examination of it by an invitation to engage in public debate. The debate was held on the campus of one of America's great universities and was widely reported in the press. In this intellectual encounter, Dr. Banowsky criticized the playboy philosophy while Anson Mount, longtime Hefner associate and Religion Editor of the magazine, attempted to uphold it. In preparation for the debate, Dr. Banowsky was Hefner's guest at the playboy mansion in Chicago, where he had opportunity to study at firsthand the many aspects of the new faith and practice. What Dr. Banowsky has discovered, and what his book shows, is that the glittering Chicago mansion symbolizes something important about our culture as a whole. This book does not, therefore, center upon such problems as pornography or obscenity, as

10

important as they may be. It centers upon ideas! It examines the way in which the current cult of pleasure distorts such basic ideals as freedom, individualism, tolerance and even pleasure itself.

Though Dr. Banowsky, as he examines the popular philosophy, concludes that it is intellectually vulnerable, he also understands its appeal. He knows that it is not completely wrong. If it were completely wrong, it would not be the threat that it now is. The author examines the different facets of the popular gospel with both sympathy and clarity. He sees that the major elements in the new faith cannot be defended and, in the light of their inadequacy, he proposes an alternative way of reaching the genuine freedom for which so many obviously hunger.

I am, personally, very glad that William S. Banowsky has taken time away from his academic responsibilities at Pepperdine College in Los Angeles to make the incisive analysis which the chapters of this book represent. He brings to this practical contemporary task both a trained mind and a compassionate heart. I am glad that he has been willing to be conspicuously honest, pointing out relentlessly the inconsistencies which he has discovered, while at the same time, he is also generous enough to mention strengths when he sees them. Above all, I am glad that his book is not merely negative and that he has had the courage to express an alternative faith which he believes is free from the criticisms he presents with such vividness. He points to One who truly calls us beyond playboy.

We shall not live responsibly in our confused time by keeping still. Because of student request, Dr. Banowsky recently participated in two significant programs in which questions relating to the new morality were vigorously discussed. James A. Pike appeared with him on one of these occasions, and Professor Joseph Fletcher on the other. We need the virility of such intellectual confrontation which can be carried on in good taste and without loss of friendship. I admire Bill Banowsky for many things, but chiefly because he is tough with ideas while he is tender with persons. I bespeak for his book a wide and thoughtful reading.

D. Elton Trueblood

It's a
Playboy
World

1.

The Distortion of the Revolution

It was the best of times,
it was the worst of times.

Charles Dickens

TODAY IT IS fashionable to speak of the moral revolution of the twentieth century, but what many people have failed to notice is that the revolution is over. In recent years, forces of another sort have taken commanding position, the very character of the upheaval has been altered decisively. The high idealism and clear-cut purposes have faded, and what was once a genuine revolution is now a mere rebellion. What it amounts to is that the moral revolution has degenerated into the cult of pleasure and the code word for the new cult is "playboy."

Inevitably, any movement loses fluidity and thrust, and when it does so, it tends to crystallize incipient ideals into a system. By this predictable pattern noble causes end up as businesses, more than a few as rackets. A contemporary illustration of this process may be drawn from developments within the American labor movement. Born of passionate desire to abolish sweatshop conditions and provide decent wages for workers, big labor itself has come to be, in some instances, exploitative; and labor bossism is now a definite part of the establishment. The difference between the sacrificial leadership of Samuel Gompers and the gangster tactics of some others is the difference between a great movement in the dynamism of youth and the corruption of old age.

Movements, like people, inevitably grow old and suffer the degenerative disease of hardening of the arteries. In more recent years, our era of protests has spawned an organization called "Proxy Pickets," which advertises that its services, in support of any kind of demonstration, may be rented by the hour. How many similar cases can be cited of humanitarian movements that accomplished their greatest good in their earliest hours, when motivating impulses were fresh, budgets were lean, and staffs were made up largely of unpaid volunteers? With success comes systematization and, not infrequently, commercialization and exploitation of the cause itself. And, in keeping with this sequence of affairs, the early-century moral revolution has become fossilized into contemporary playboyism. Sensualism is the easy vice of young men and old civilizations.

When corruption sets in, the lofty ideals that gave birth to a movement are soon lost sight of, or, worse still, subject to perversion. We must remember that any good is easily perverted and, as a rule, the greater the good the greater the resulting evil. Unfortunately, the greatest truths are the easiest to pervert.

The French Revolution is a classic illustration of the shocking way in which liberal ideas may be diverted into illiberal practices. The glorification of liberty, equality, and fraternity was only a short step from the crashing sound of the guillotine. And Charles Dickens began *A Tale of Two Cities,* with his paradox: "It was the best of times, it was the worst of times." With amazing rapidity, the "spring of hope" turned to "the winter of despair."

In more recent years, Nazism emerged through exploitation of the philosophy of Friedrich Nietzsche. While we hold little esteem for Nietzsche's egoistic materialism, we are sure that he would have been the first to resist the distortion of his idea of the superman into the ruthless politics of Hitler. Though

Nietzsche despised German nationalism, a calculated exploitation of his fierce philosophy prepared the way for Hitler's bloodbath.

And today, we are witnessing a basic distortion of the lofty ideals that characterized the moral revolution of the twentieth century. Freedom, tolerance, individualism, happiness—each is good, but not unqualifiedly good, because each may be perverted. Although we hear as much as ever about these values, the original idealism has largely vanished, and the words sound like weary clichés. How ironic that the high-minded enthusiasm that erupted to correct the evils of an ecclesiastical establishment has been siphoned off to serve the commercial interests of a massive establishment of pleasure.

Future historians may well be amazed when they examine the process by which a set of truly revolutionary ideas, based on human compassion, was accommodated to support what is fundamentally a doctrine of self-centeredness. Everybody knows that self-centeredness is not new, but many people do not realize that neither was the term "playboy" originated by its present promoters. The word was first popularized by Irish playwright John Millington Synge, in 1907, when it took rare moral courage to challenge the inconsistencies of the old morality. His rollicking comedy, *The Playboy of the Western World*, was banned by Boards of Guardians in Irish towns; it caused riotous demonstrations when it was staged in London; and in Philadelphia, the entire Abbey Theatre Company was arrested under the MacNichol Law, aimed at the prevention of "lascivious, sacreligious, obscene, or indecent plays." Now we read the play with amusement, wondering what all the commotion was about; but it was strong stuff in its own day, and a prologue for something more. The original *Playboy* appeared on the early winds of the movement that was soon to rise to gale proportions and would eventually be known as the moral revolution of the twentieth century.

Synge's bold attempt at realism, his gay defiance of Victorian convention, his demand that men deal honestly with life as it is rather than as priests and preachers made it out to be, proved to be foundation stones for the new moral structure. Irish Catholics felt that Synge had misrepresented them, had ridiculed the manners and morals of their nation.

"... I have used one or two words only that I have not heard among the country people of Ireland...." Synge answered, in his published preface to *The Playboy of the Western World*. "...Anyone who has lived in real intimacy with the Irish peasantry will know that the wildest sayings and ideas in this play are tame indeed, compared with the fancies one may hear in any little hillside cabin in Geesala, or Carraroe, or Dingle Bay."

Among those who came to his aid, were George Bernard Shaw and William Butler Yeats, who insisted that Synge was merely "telling it like it was," and charged that this was precisely why the prim people were shocked. "The Playboy's real name was Synge, and the famous libel on Ireland was the truth about the world," wrote Shaw in the Irish Supplement of the *New Statesman* of July 12, 1913. Yeats said that the reaction bared a nation so inhibited by religious pretense that it was unwilling to face the truth and bitterly wrote the poem "On Those That Hated 'The Playboy of the Western World' 1907."

It is a long way from John Millington Synge's three-act play to Hugh Hefner's 300,000 word bible, *The Playboy Philosophy*, but that suggests how far we have come in the first seventy years of our century. Much of the ground covered represents genuine gain, but a lie is never so dangerous as when it is woven into a fabric of truth. Hugh Hefner has a wide popular following for much the same reason that George Wallace was so successful politically. Both men have spoken out clearly and loudly on crucial and frequently neglected issues and what they have said has contained much truth. Above all, they have put their messages into simplistic terms, and reduced complex issues into simple formulas. The characteristic disciples of both men frequently exclaim of their leaders, "In any case, he's honest; he tells it like it is; he really lets 'em have it." But the gospel according to playboy is conspicuously untrue. In the name of realism, this popular philosophy seems to be lying about life. The pleasure prophets are not genuine iconoclasts; they have appropriated the vocabulary of the moral revolution without paying the price paid by Synge and his colleagues. Today the use of the word "playboy" requires no moral courage at all, and is a pathway to popularity rather than to persecution.

In the interest of historical perspective, let's look at some of the circumstances that produced this contemporary cult. The simple pursuit of pleasure is a way of life that filled in the ethical vacuum created by the collapse of religion and its moral sanctions. Ours is not the first age to experience the dissolution of an old faith, nor is it the first in which no vital new faith has come forth to fill the awful void. It is history's habit that one generation's heterodoxy becomes the next generation's orthodoxy and that, when the time is full, the newer orthodoxy requires replacement by fresh convictions that will provide a new basis for moral order. It is absurd to imagine that we are the first to live with change. But the changes of our time have been so sweeping and fundamental—the old order has been so thoroughly wrecked—that the new convictions have not yet crystallized and no definite order seems to be arising from the ashes of the old. Why? Because what has been demolished is not merely the faith of the previous generation but the spiritual structure of many centuries and with it have passed the compelling reasons which certified morality itself.

The unique feature of the present moral crisis is not so much a more widespread violation of standards as it is the rejection of the idea that there are any. When has any age been free of widespread violation of its accepted code? Was the age of

Puritanism really any freer? The records of the Boston Church show that of the two hundred persons owning the baptismal covenant there from 1760 to 1775, sixty-six confessed to fornication before marriage. In all types of disciplinary cases listed in the records of Massachusetts' churches, a majority of them confessed fornication. To transgress accepted values is one thing, but to lose all sense of an objective moral order is quite another, and this is precisely our predicament. And it is why any analysis of the present crisis that spends its time comparing the immorality in our time with that of previous generations fails to connect. Whether there is now a greater incidence of sexual promiscuity than ever is not the central question. What *is* important is that so many are asking: "So what if we do have sex outside of marriage! Who's to say that there's anything wrong with it?"

But few have been made truly happy by the new freedom. Walk the streets of any city and see how many happy faces you observe. What seems to distinguish our generation is not mere rebellion against our parents' religion and moral code, but deep disillusionment with our own rebellion. We are attempting to live in a moral vacuum that has no precedence in Western civilization. Belief in the stern Calvinistic God has faded forever and most men sense a deep loss of inward conviction; they are convinced they will never be so sure again. Values which seemed absolute have been desacralized; decisions once so clear-cut have been relativized; and simple ethical certainty, of the sort once available to the average man, has gone. To a few, such boundless freedom may be exhilarating, but to more ordinary men the impact is devastating.

Ours may well be the first generation in the history of mankind when cataclysmic events of the age have so united with the prevailing intellectual mood as to render any absolute or authoritative belief incredible to large masses of men. Others before us have known unsettling effects of crisis and war but, in our time, these effects are proving both devastating and worldwide. We conduct our daily affairs with the knowledge that intercontinental ballistic missiles, armed with nuclear warheads, are pinpointed on major cities of East and West. What a terrible irony that our generation, whose grandfathers fought the war to end all wars in 1917, is the first generation required to live all of its years under the instant prospect of global annihilation. The early-century optimism, which now seems quaint, has given way to a deep sense of futility. Our mood of utter despair stems from a recognition of the vast difference between where we are now and where we were supposed to have been by now. As Jean-Paul Sartre sadly concludes: There is no exit from the human dilemma.

Today, there is a pervasive mood of impermanence, especially among very young people. Many express the feeling that time is running out, that there are but a few years left in which to experience the full measure of life. One youngster, likening cold-war brinkmanship to stereotyped TV cowboy duels, said matter-of-factly: "I wonder how long the big guns will stay holstered!" To many, it seems to be but a matter of time. At first, this sense of impending doom led to a post-war surge in church attendance which, for a passing moment, looked like a revival of religion. Billy Graham's meteoric ministry was launched during this period and no sermon was more central to his message than that on eschatology—the end of the world. For several years, people rushed back to the sanctuaries and scrambled into the coliseum rallies in droves. But the so-called religious renaissance, which was never really widespread or deep, is certainly over; and it was, in some aspects, a momentary form of escape. The tense years are turning into decades and the easiest anesthesia to deaden the constant ache of emptiness is proving to be the simple pursuit of pleasure.

When men lose their sense of established standards, they

21

tend to fall victim to an urge for pleasure or a lust for power. And when the loss of standards occurs during a period of peril, men seem to prefer pleasure to power. It is one of the sad facts of war that the specter of danger and death causes many soldiers to want to spend the evening before the terrible battle with the prostitute rather than the priest. It has been said that there are more brothels in Saigon, today, than in any other city of comparable size in the world.

In *The Plague,* a novel that serves as a parable of our times, Albert Camus pictures a North African city under siege by a devastating epidemic of bubonic plague. When the initial wave of panic begins to subside, Camus describes the surprising response of the populace: "But once the people realized their instant peril, they gave their thoughts to pleasure. All the hideous fears that stamp their faces in the daytime are transformed in the fiery, dusty nightfall into a sort of hectic exaltation, an unkempt freedom fevering their blood."

Camus has painted the desperation of our post-Hiroshima world, and the-eat-drink-and-be-merry-for-tomorrow-we-may-die spirit, which always accompanies a nation's young men to the fighting front, has settled about the world because the world has become the battlefront. Violent tides have swept some from confusion into despair, and from despair into meaningless self-indulgence. There is evidence that millions may now be living, primarily, to satisfy the needs of the moment. Having lost any real sense of idealistic lift, are we becoming creatures of pleasure? Frank Sinatra has been quoted as confirming Camus' poetic insight by reducing the real-life resignation of the times to a pitiful phrase: "I'm for anything that gets you through the night, be it prayer, pills, or a bottle of Jack Daniels." If, for any considerable number, just getting through the long night is such a genuine struggle, what a terrible commentary on our civilization.

There is always profit in confusion, for with the loss of

meaning and inner direction, come the legion of looters. Just as the closing days of the civil war drew carpetbaggers into the beleagured South, the waning of the moral revolution has brought moral carpetbaggers to fill the vacuum caused by the dissolution of all that once was. The goods for disguising pain and creating the sensation of pleasure are in abundant supply, because America and the Americanized countries of Western Europe are enjoying a period of unparalleled affluence. Our economy of plenty has produced a culture of consumption and leisure. Though millions are plagued by poverty and remain insecure, the average man enjoys a living standard which, a century earlier, would have been the envy of the Queen of England. Never have so many families had so much money beyond the margin of necessity and never have they had more free time in which to spend it. The climate of emptiness, fear, and affluence is ripe for exploitation.

Commerce and industry have been quick to respond, and the flood of mass-produced creature comforts is topped only by Madison Avenue's finesse in advertising them. Much of the best intelligence in our society is devoted to money-making. No one overtly twists the customer's arm, but propaganda and persuasion—both blatant and subliminal—insult his manhood and threaten his employment, his community status and his sex appeal, unless he smokes the right cigarette and reclines in the right easy chair in the right style home in the right neighborhood. The appeal is to gratification of every physical desire, relief of every pain; and the vehicle used for the big sale is sex. Razor blades, refrigerators, automobiles—almost everything being manufactured—is hawked by sultry-voiced, erotically-positioned, scantily-clad females. One manufacturer has brought out a line of brassieres with foam rubber bosoms, for little girls of ten.

When the time for fullest exploitation of human emptiness was exactly right, technology gave us the vast wasteland—a medium for tubing titillation into our living rooms. Television commercials have abandoned all pretense at subtlety: One wine advertisement features a sexy-looking woman asking, "Had any lately?" Another manufacturer has its sex-symbol proposition, "You get a *lot* more than smoke with our cigar!" And, of course, the shaving cream peddled by the seductive *femme fatale* writhing to the tune of "The Stripper" and exhorting, "Take it off, take it *all* off!" Sex, as anyone who sits through an evening of television or thumbs through a magazine knows, is the cornerstone of mass persuasion and the symbol *par excellence* of the life of leisure and consumption.

The movie industry continues to strengthen its offerings in order to earn its share of the take in this rush to capitalize on the consumer—the man with his moral pants down. During the 'forties and 'fifties, the Code of the Motion Picture Association of America was demolished, but that was merely the beginning. The content of violence, promiscuity, and homosexuality increases precipitously with each new film, keeping pace with public tastes. People are looking for something with a kick— for fun, for vicarious thrills—and producers are pleased to give them whatever they are willing to pay for.

The publishing industry also plays a major role both in the reflection and extension of the pursuit of pleasure. Hardcore pornography is a multimillion dollar a year business, but even the advertising pages of the most sedate journals implore people to buy a certain toothpaste because it gives your mouth sex appeal. It was entirely in keeping with the nature of things when America's largest circulated women's monthly magazine decorated its cover with bold, black letters asking, "Is Adultery Ever Justified?", prominently adding as a come-on the spicy subtitle: "Bishop Pike's Startling New Answer to an Old Dilemma!"

In the struggle to find reasonable answers to hard questions, a distinction must be drawn between that approach which, no matter how unorthodox, treasures responsibility and good taste and that which exploits sensationalism. When the clergy must enter the fray, one should hope that it would be in a truly responsible hunt for solutions rather than headlines.

Men of many professions have gotten in on the act. In the field of medicine an extraordinary new breed has developed— the professional sexologist. The high priest of this trade is Dr. Albert Ellis who practices psychotherapy in Manhattan and writes books dedicated to liberating our repressed society from the clutches of Victorianism. A Ph.D. from Columbia University, his half-dozen scintillating paperbacks (which bill him as America's foremost authority on sex) are perennial favorites at any neighborhood newsstand. One of his top sellers is *Sex and the Single Man* which features chapters on "The Art of Seduction," "What Every Young Man Should Know About Bedmanship," "How to Avoid Venereal Disease," "Consumer's Guide to Prostitution," and "How to Be Happy Though Married." Dr. Ellis, although more financially successful than most, is but one example of that army of writers who assure us that happiness is a fuller sex life, a better grade of wall-to-wall carpet, a longer cigarette, a trip to Acapulco.

One of the most determined proponents of pleasure-seeking is Hugh Hefner. Starting on a shoestring in 1955, with a center-page foldout of a nude Marilyn Monroe, he has parlayed the playboy theme into a multimillion-dollar empire— one of the most amazing financial success stories in journalistic history. Although he was ignored at the outset as publisher of yet another girlie book, Hefner's ambitions were higher than that and his unique instincts and capacity for hard work have proved equal to his ambitions. He timed to perfection the swing of Western civilization through the moral revolution and aimed his magazine at the very outer edge of that swing, while gingerly remaining within acceptable bounds for majority tastes. From the first, he committed himself to high editorial standards, he paid top fees to attract big-name writers, explored vital social and political topics, and clung so tenaciously to the vanguard that he has achieved the enviable reputation of being, not a mere reflector of change, but its actual producer. He is, however, essentially a reflection and that is why he cannot be taken casually. He speaks to almost twenty million readers every month and, on the American campus, as something of an oracle. Aside from the *Reader's Digest,* which has a considerable edge in age and the advantage of being printed in several languages, *Playboy* is the most widely circulated American magazine in all of Western Europe.

If anyone is qualified to give the official statement for this contemporary cult, it is Hugh Hefner. This he has done, with a twenty-five installment editorial series spanning a two-year period and named, appropriately, *The Playboy Philosophy.* Hefner is important, more as a reflection of the present mood of our society than as a cause. It is not his flirtation with pornography—what Mort Sahl calls girls who fold in two places and wear staples in their navels—that concerns us, it is his life philosophy. What is deserving of social comment is the intent of *Playboy* magazine, not the content.

We do not use *The Playboy Philosophy* as a handy whipping boy but, since it expresses the most popular and definitive statements on the subject, it serves to symbolize the perversion of the revolution. If it reflected merely one man's, or one magazine's, point of view it would be of slight importance. While there is no way to determine exactly, there is every reason to suspect that Hefner's life-style is representative of the mood of millions. Many who have never read his philosophy and who would disavow it if they did so, tend to confirm it by the pattern of their lives. Many of the American middle-class, in a practical way, are deeply implicated in the playboy drift.

Life magazine says that more than forty billion dollars a

year is spent on the pursuit of pleasure, an amount greater than is spent on education and religion combined. Using this measurement of the way we live rather than the values to which we pay lip service, there is a good likelihood that, of all contemporary spokesmen, the one who speaks for the largest segment of Western civilization is Hugh Hefner.

Hefner and other prophets of playboyism are neither originators or perpetuators of the moral revolution; they are exploiters of it. When the revolutionary movement won its original objectives and began to wane, these opportunists, who had been waiting in the wings, moved at once to center stage. Their major strategy is to create the illusion that the battle is joined: the threat from Victorian convention is still very real. But what they are fighting is a position no serious body of opinion now maintains. Long after the caricatured Puritan code has been laid to rest, they continue to scrutinize and castigate it as though it were the supreme danger menacing mankind. It is interesting to conjecture how a real Puritan, such as John Milton, might have handled them.

It is amazing that such an attack upon what is really a straw man has won such a wide public following. While it is surprising that anybody could ever have believed that masturbation causes hepatitis, it is far more surprising that men should still be building financially rewarding careers out of campaigning against such historic trivia. How strange that men should struggle with myths nobody any longer believes and warn of superstitions and taboos that have not been live options for years. They find it highly profitable to evangelize against sexual taboos as outdated as the old-fashioned corset, quoting at length ludicrous passages from nineteenth century sex manuals as though such quaint tidbits were inhibiting contemporary mores. They persist in preaching Freudian gospel of the 1920's, as though the central sickness of our permissive society is sexual inhibitions and hang-ups.

Why do so many buy their belated propaganda? Because many continue to be nostalgic about an old morality, even though they no longer practice it.

The old morality was in need of renovation, but it had its better side, and we have discarded the total fabric too indiscriminately. But what resulted from its worst side was a brand of ethical legalism that trivialized morality and encouraged glaring inconsistencies. Its system sought cheap escape from the agonizing decisions of life by reducing ethical decisions to a series of arbitrary regulations. It tended to be concerned about the sacredness of persons only in the second instance; its first loyalty was given over to fastidious observance of prearranged rules. *Sex* was the unpardonable sin, but flagrant acts of greed, pride, and discrimination barely made the list. Sexual sin usually meant that one had to go all the way. Consequently a girl could be fondled regularly and thoroughly, but she preserved her purity if she stopped short of the magic line that holds the fragile gem of virginity technically intact. The old morality permitted a businessman to exploit his employees, yet appear righteous if he neither smoked nor drank. It allowed a salesman to be shady, if not downright dishonest, in his professional techniques, provided he kept his morals intact by being faithful to his wife. It condoned the ruthless pursuit of money, provided the pursuer was successful and placed a proper share in the offering plate. It forbade the use of four-letter words, but giggled when pious white people contemptuously called other human beings "niggers." We may be grateful to the moral revolution for exposing this attitude long ago and for banishing forever the notion that righteousness may be cut down to manageable size by memorizing a sheet of do's and don'ts.

One reason the prophets of pleasure-seeking have been successful in fighting the shadow of a finished revolution is that a small segment of society still clings to the old morality and provides some semblance of a valid target. This group is committing a colossal tactical blunder, because it is providing the playboys with a counter extreme crucial to the success of their campaign. A few religious leaders remain aloof from reality, refusing to grant the ground won by the moral revolution and forfeiting the right to be taken seriously. Earnest men, understandably perplexed by the confused shape of things, they nonetheless waste their energies perpetuating an irrelevant battle. Without respect for denominational lines, they are scattered throughout the churches. The ones who occupy pulpits devote the large part of their ministries to being against things and to answering tired questions no one is asking. When parishioners come from spiritually-starved worlds in search of Sunday bread, they are given stones instead. Why else are thousands ceasing to come? It is possible for the church, one of the wealthiest institutions on earth, to deceive itself with a gaudy show of Sunday-morning strength, yet no longer operate as a genuine power in contemporary affairs. Modern men neither cherish the church nor persecute it; they simply ignore it! It is looked upon as something with marginal relevance, a nice place to marry off one's daughters or to bury one's dead. One of the clearest lessons of history is that a faith may appear to continue or even flourish long after its real vitality is gone.

Because of the spiritual vacuum, it has been easy for playboyism to come forward as the new authority—the new cult or religion. History reveals that every upheaval—religious or social—which sets out to exorcise old authority, invariably ends in the acknowledgment of some new authority. The playboy philosophy is really the revival of paganism. It purports to be the truth about the world which shall make men free. "My great religion is a belief in the blood, the flesh, as being wiser than the intellect," writes D. H. Lawrence. "We can go wrong with our minds, but what our blood feels and believes and

Revival of Paganism

says is always true." Then, adds the author of *Lady Chatterley's Lover*, "The real way of living is to answer one's wants."

The relativization of values that has occurred in our time will lead some men into a constructive maturity, but it will send others into ethical anarchism. In *The Secular City*, Harvey Cox observes that when relativization of values produces a dizzy descent toward nihilism, it leads squarely into the arms of a new and tribal cult, back into "a value system with its own idols and icons, even if they appear as gargoyles." The idol of playboyism is unabashed pleasure; and its most avid worshipers are fresh converts who use their new-found freedom from the restrictions of the old code to revel in all the ways of abandon that the dead code forbade, not to become truly free men. This preoccupation with attacking an old idol produces its own new idol, and casting out old demons can itself be a consuming commitment.

The success of the playboy cult, perhaps more than any other recent phenomenon, dramatizes this conformity syndrome in our society. What parades itself about as rugged individualism is actually a sign of inner estrangement and outer conformity. One does not become a genuine individualist merely by separating himself from the traditional pattern. Every generation produces subculture reactionaries, who make a big thing of absolute individuality. In the effort to avoid resembling others, they end up duplicating the dress, jargon, and value system of other members of the estranged group. Standing apart from others may or may not be necessary to assert true individualism, but to depart from others with no higher purpose than to be different from the norm is a purely negative reaction.

Inhabitors of the pages of the cult's most popular mouthpiece are fantasy creatures known as playboys and bunnies. Everyone dresses alike, talks alike, eats alike and has his own key to the Kingdom. As further security, bunny ears are

30

stamped on cufflinks, wallets, golfclubs, shirts, and a score of other mass-produced gadgets. This empire grossed two and one-half million dollars last year selling such status symbols. Particularly revealing is "The Playboy Forum," which yields the definitive word about the "in" cologne, the right wine, the proper way to carry off a seduction. The picture one gets is not of an ebullient individualist, but of a nervous suburbanite, who seems to be worried about the crease in his pants or the part in his hair. To mimic selfhood by such eccentricity is really a total surrender to the judgment of others.

The playboy is a professional parasite feeding upon the perpetual destruction of the fallen Puritan idol. As he goes forth to conquer chastity, self-denial, Priscilla Alden, and the Southern Baptist Convention, he embraces the very demons with which he wrestles. They furnish him, by inversion, with a kind of religious assurance and point of focus that enables him to think he is doing exactly as he pleases. Actually, however, his very freedom from ancient taboos renders him credulous to new ones. He is emancipated from past prejudices only to be victimized by contemporary ones. His is not the thoroughgoing relativism it appears to be, but a rigid value system. Many modern men have submitted to a new form of haughty authoritarianism that dictates their attitudes and conduct.

What is the answer to the moral crisis of our time? A rebirth of the moral revolution! We must reject the playboy trend as a diversion and discover once again that pathway of high commitment to ethical purpose on which so much earlier progress was achieved. Just as the original revolution was a judgment against the rigidities of the old religion, we must ignite another moral movement as a judgment against the simplifications of this new religion. If the old religion involved a refusal to accept the whole truth about the world, the new denomination is even more delusive, because the purposeless pursuit of pleasure is essentially escapist. It represents a desperate effort to avoid the pain of being a whole person in our kind of world.

The good news is that many of the young people in our society are preparing for a return to the revolution. Their restless mood and their refusal to accept on a chrome platter what was supposed to have been "The Great Society" is the world's best hope for a better tomorrow. We must reject as utterly false the prevailing idea that this activist generation is wild and ungrateful, hell-bent on destroying Western civilization. If our society is to be saved at all, it will be by the deep moral concern of youth. There is much confusion but: When was any generation ever more compulsively honest and idealistic? When was any generation more determined to discover for themselves values that are worth the investment of their lives?

What are those values to which this generation should give commitment? The pathetic fact is that our young people have been given confused leadership. The prophets of the new paganism appeal to the young because they appear to be idealistic, but that appearance is grossly deceiving. These men are not really revolutionaries but priests in the new establishment. Deeply entrenched in the institutions of society, they dominate much of its commercial enterprise. The professional playboys are men who escaped from a stale orthodoxy in their own youth, yet found no new commitment to replace the old. Perhaps, there was a time when they were authentic revolutionaries, but they gave up on changing the world long ago and went into the business of exploiting it instead.

Is it the pattern of history that today's revolutionaries become tomorrow's shopkeepers? Is it necessary that the moral dynamism of the "now" generation be drained off, and splendid young people must become keepers of another establishment that appears to encourage a fresh vision but, in actuality, preaches an old tired gospel already obsolete in ancient Greece?

During an earlier period of confusion, Walter Lippmann's *A Preface to Morals* expressed the spirit of our present task. "The true business of the moralist in the midst of all this," he said, "is to see as clearly as he can into the meaning of it, so that out of the chaos of pain and happiness and worry he may help to deliver a usable insight." Because the moral confusion of our time is an ideological confusion we cannot find our way unless we begin to think more deeply about ideas that have been distorted. Those very values that form the foundation of Western civilization—freedom, necessity for tolerance, the worth and dignity of the individual and his rights of life, liberty, and the pursuit of happiness—are what cause our present confusion for these are also the major themes the prophets of pleasure have stressed. There is no doubt about the desirability of these objectives, but how are these objectives to be realized?

We have good reason to be highly suspicious of the pleasure-seeking method. Aristotle was perhaps the first to point out that one could best judge the validity of a philosophy by examining its fruits. You do not know a philosophy in its genesis, you know it in its final product. The gospel according to playboy is not producing what it has promised. If we were a poverty-stricken people we might be able to convince ourselves that the good life consists of pleasures and comforts— having plenty of everything. But we have been on that trail long enough to know that it leads nowhere; we must find a better way.

If we have any intellectual sophistication we are aware that the alternative to one error may be another error. The fact that a harsh moral position is evil does not convince us that an opposite stance of mere permissiveness is in itself good. Both may be evil and available evidence points to the conclusion that both *are* evil. There is no liberation in escaping from one bondage only to be signed up as devout believers and practicing members of the pleasure establishment. There must be a third way, and it is our task to engage in hard thinking in the hope of finding it.

2.

The Paradox of Pleasure

The pursuit of happiness was always a most unhappy quest.
Walter Lippmann

PLEASURE is a good thing. All else being equal it is much
better to enjoy what is pleasant than to endure what is mis-
erable. What is strange is that so many assume, uncritically,
that because pleasure is good, it is the primary good—even the
only good. It is the way of life for millions, and is the un-
stated and unargued assumption of those who advertise and
those who respond to the advertisements.

When Sean Flynn, son of late actor Errol Flynn, asked a
Santa Monica court recently, "What's so wrong, nowadays,
with a young man specializing in pleasure?" he was parroting
an old question with far-reaching philosophical implications.
The question of pleasure and its place in the good life is an
ancient one. The trappings of each era change, but the essential human situation remains the same. Every generation
tends to believe that its circumstances are novel, and our present preoccupation in defending or attacking the pursuit of
pleasure makes us lose sight of the enduring nature of the
pleasure question. Some, like Flynn and his father, are content
to ask, "What's so wrong . . . ?" assuming that to ask such a
question will somehow justify their brand of irresponsible
living. They seek to avoid the intellectual effort required to
answer their own question. But more thoughtful men have

been led to ask the prior question: "What do you mean by pleasure?"

Hedonism, the broad ethical term for all theories of philosophy in which the ultimate criterion for conduct is pleasure, has had notable defenders, both in antiquity and in modern times. It is a formidable moral philosophy, and its perennial plausibility is forged from the irresistible fact that *pleasure is good;* so good that all normal people instinctively and universally desire it. The inherent value of pleasure is unmistakable. When a person claims that he has done what is true or what is beautiful, we may disagree. But if he says that what he has done is pleasurable we take it to mean that he knows what he is talking about. Other values that may be called good appear less tangible and more difficult to define, but the value of pleasure seems to be undeniable, regardless of its subjective nature. When one experiences pleasantness one seems to be experiencing good itself, not just something which accompanies good; when one experiences the opposite—pain— one seems to be experiencing bad itself. The playboy doctrine thus seems to begin with a *prima facie* claim to reasonableness.

The long history of hedonism is checkered with diverse schools of thought concerning the ways and means of human pleasure, but the schools hold in common the belief that pleasure *is* the ultimate good. What compounds the confusion of our present moral crisis is that our generation is largely ignorant of the doctrine's development in the history of human thought. Many of our contemporaries are remarkably naïve, in that their interpretation of human nature is as sentimental and unreal as Puritanism ever was. They believe that life is a simple matter of black and white, that the meaning of human happiness can be boiled down to the vulgar formula, "Everybody ought to do his own thing!" Virtually none of the philosophers who have taken the pleasure principle as the criterion for conduct would accept this colloquial definition.

Those that neglect history are doomed to repeat it. Contemporary pleasure-seekers seem to be unfamiliar with the hard lesson of the past—happiness is a paradox. Part of the wisdom of the ages is that the best way to get happiness is to forget about it.

The popular idea of pleasure has two indivisible components: *sensuality* and *immediacy*. Though this definition is clearly implicit in many television commercials and magazine advertisements, we also have the benefit of formal statements. Among the books published by Allen Ginzberg, who was convicted on a pornography charge upheld by the Supreme Court, is the *Housewife's Handbook on Selective Promiscuity*. Author Rey Anthony of Oakland, California, also conducts sexual seminars for housewives. "Hedonism," says Miss Anthony, "is sensual pleasure and something that you just can't do one night and have hangovers the next day and regrets and guilt and shame and everything like that. I mean, the thing about sensual pleasure is that it is just pleasurable in and by itself." The same clarity characterizes the Pagans, a motorcycle group in the Washington area that corresponds to California's Hell's Angels. "I have tried marriage, and the home and the kids and it ain't hitting on nothin'," one of them explained. "What I like about the Pagans is that every night you can get drunk, have a blast, and enjoy yourself. Broads and booze and everything they got to offer." The current motto appears to be the maxim from Aldous Huxley's *Brave New World:* "Never put off until tomorrow the fun you can have today."

It would be absurd to suggest that the average American housewife is planning adventures in promiscuity or that many men are thinking of joining rebellious motorcycle gangs, but these statements are far more representative than they appear. This is because hedonism is not a specific set of acts, but a philosophy of life—an attitude toward pleasure—which is widely shared by those who may not demonstrate it in harsh, unconventional ways. Preoccupation with the pursuit of pleasure is not limited to a few social rebels or fashionable bums; the respectable middle-class is deeply implicated. As Mr. Hefner notes in *The Playboy Philosophy*, a playboy can be a university professor, a worker in the arts, a sharp-minded young executive, an architect, an engineer, "providing he possesses a certain *point of view*. He must see life not as a vale of tears, but as a happy time ... a man sensitive to pleasure, a man who—without acquiring the stigma of the voluptuary or dilettante—can live life to the hilt. This is the sort of man we mean when we use the word *playboy*."

Never before have so many men been given an opportunity to put this definition to the test under such favorable circumstances. Hefner's general concept requires that a successful playboy have freedom from want and fear, sufficient material means to pursue whatever pleases him, and the ability to do so without worrying about any religious or social reprisals. Prior to our time these requirements were difficult to meet, so the standard stereotype of the pleasure-seeker was the well-to-do Bohemian. Now the barriers have been eliminated and the older image no longer holds.

If the twentieth century is the time, the modern city is the place for the middle-class pleasure cult. The pleasure cults of Greece and Rome had a hard time convincing even a few citizens that the gods were really dead, but modern urban men have inherited a metaphysics by which they believe their deeds to be beyond the concern of any all-seeing eye. In *The Summing Up* Somerset Maugham tells how he ceased to believe in God when he "felt the exhilaration of a new freedom." Some may be shocked by the report that "God is dead," but millions of modern men go about business as usual because they were never concerned with God anyway.

Playboys of earlier days were also buffeted by countless physical consequences, but such barriers as infection and conception have been removed by modern medicine and contraceptives. The present pleasure cult appeals to men who have been relieved of social inhibitions. In the past, the hedonist was often an outcast, a man of doubtful reputation standing against the *status quo.* Classical hedonism faded with the advent of Christianity because the message of self-denial provided an unfavorable climate for all egoistic philosophies. This meant that from the first century until the present one, most hedonists were men willing to be branded as social rebels. In the seventeenth century, for example, Thomas Hobbes shocked his generation by teaching that man is totally selfish and should seek his own advantage; our present climate is cordial to his philosophy.

Just as the new metaphysics has freed many men from the fear of God, the urban style of life has delivered them from interference by their neighbors. Millions live in apartment houses where everybody is expected to mind his own business, or in tidy subdivisions where fences wall in the backyard barbecue and wall out the next-door neighbor. A husband who has extramarital designs may take a thirty-minute drive down the freeway and off the ramp into anonymity, where choices are more numerous than if he had landed among amorous natives on a remote island. The real danger does not reside in the freedom of urbanization *per se,* but the low uses to which many have put it. Anonymity and mobility are not inherently negative, they are necessary ingredients in the urban social system. They provide immunity from endless distraction and opportunity for selectivity in relationships and activities apart from which meaningful personal life in any large city is impossible. Anonymity need not mean depersonalization; it may afford the high privilege of privacy and the opportunity to concentrate upon really worthwhile relationships. And mobility need not be mere movement, it can be the means to enriching versatility and the possibility for greater personal and professional fulfillment. The freedom of urbanization is the challenge to create a quality and variety of life never before possible. But not all men are prepared to live with freedom. For some men, the style of urban life is an invitation to mediocrity. The same freeway that goes past the library leads also to the topless bar.

In addition to religious and social inhibitions, men of earlier times were restrained from pursuing the pleasure impulses because not many of them could afford the price. All the wisdom of the ages seems to establish a direct connection between prosperity and the pursuit of pleasure. In the words of Cotton Mather, "Piety begat prosperity and the daughter divorced the mother." Since the end of the second world war, affluence has given millions both time and means to seek the prerequisites of pleasure, which once seemed available only to the very rich. Striking evidence of this is afforded by recent developments in Western Europe, especially in London. Despite the serious economic crisis, the British have never lived so well, and the style of the good life, the pleasurable life, is being adapted by members of the working class. Young adults have more money than ever before and they are spending it on whatever pleases them. London hair styles and habits of dress, once so formal, now ignore social and class distinctions and, to a marked degree, blur sexual distinctions as well. In recent years the United States has ceased to influence and has begun to imitate British dress and mod manners. It is an arresting possibility that young adults in Britain are even more pleasure-conscious than their American counterparts. Although Western Europe still lags behind America in seeking pleasure through the use of narcotics, they seem to evidence an even greater measure of sexual license.

Because the pleasure cult is inherently materialistic, it is readily tied to the acquisitive instinct—to the making and spending of money. Television and magazine advertising remind us constantly that the good life is an endless tour from haberdashery to hair stylist, from bowling alley to golf course. Because advertising is, by definition, the organized effort to extend and intensify desire, its effectiveness is frightening. Last year, by a sheer avalanche of advertising, American men were enticed to purchase almost one-third of all articles sold in the toiletries and cosmetic industry—a business once patronized almost entirely by women. Success is sometimes measured in terms of the goods and services a man can purchase. In an atmosphere of unencumbered leisure and mechanical comfort, sexual desirability is pictured as the pathway to upward mobility. Sex is the status symbol of the good life.

This distorted vision may be partially responsible for the frustrations associated with the war on poverty. In early analysis of the urban crisis many were led to believe that the problem could be solved by transferring some of the goods and gadgets from the suburb to the ghetto. Bitter experience has taught us that the crisis in the ghetto goes much deeper than material possessions. We cannot share what we do not have, and the truly frightening prospect arises not from the physical and material gulf that separates the ghetto from the suburb, but from the absence of life-purpose, which traps both in a common disillusionment. The external differences of the two worlds remain unforgivably great, but any solution that focuses upon external treatment only will misfire. As Daniel Moynihan's report indicated, the heart of the ghetto crisis is the breakdown in family life. It is easier to construct apartment houses than to build families, easier to put up schools than to create a compelling desire to learn. Sensitive black leaders see this and shout back, "Physician, heal thyself!" The growing refusal of Afro-Americans to become carbon copies of the amorphous white middle-class and their insistence upon achieving their own sense of dignity is perhaps the nearest thing to a saving mission and sense of purpose now demon-

41

strated in the American democracy. Let us hope that it will not degenerate into a pursuit of the good life as television commercials picture it.

In *The Couples,* John Updike shows the deep involvement of the middle class in the pleasure cult. The time is today, the place the fictitious but all too familiar community of Tarbox, Massachusetts. The disturbingly believable characters are not bizarre Bohemians or jaded gigolos; they are a contractor, a dentist, a biochemist, a shop foreman, and housewives who live in every middle-class, American suburb. In an average town of ordinary people, the couples are caught up in a playboy binge with recreational sex as the favorite indoor sport. There are whiskey-driven parties by night and elaborate weekend rendezvous; by day women gossip, in the gay, empty tones of bourgeois life. The style is one of debonaire guiltlessness as the half-dozen housewives swap their husbands in and out of bed with an irresistible why-not willingness.

Is it all fantastic, too sensational? One of Updike's characters sums it up thus: "We're a subversive cell, like in the catacombs. Only they were trying to break out of hedonism. We're trying to break back into it. It's not easy." Allowing for obvious overdrawing, Updike's picture of things may be all too real. The mood in these contemporary catacombs is boredom, disillusionment that leads to a desperate attempt to summon joy into an otherwise meaningless life. Millions of ordinary people, as sincerely shocked by the couples of Tarbox as they are distressed by their own son's experimentation with dope or their daughter's with sex, are the real backbone of today's pleasure cult. Who buys the barren books, subsidizes the movies, demands the frothy television diet? Who makes the easy-credit, expense-account economy, which exotic restaurants, country clubs and night spots accept greedily? How has life come to mean a boat at the seashore, season tickets on the fifty-yard line, a massage and steam at the club?

And what about the young executives who sprout ulcers as they dash full speed to pay for the patio and pool and last year's trip to the Bahamas? What of the paunchy gourmets who, while they take self-righteous pride in abstention from drinking and fornicating, are exquisitely exact in their eating? Calories and cholesterol have become national enemies, and health clinics and exercising spas promising the body beautiful abound. We overeat, oversex, overplay. Why do we remain empty, insecure and bored?

The best cure for hedonism is to try to practice it, as Updike illustrates. In a sense *The Couples* is a happy-ending book—everybody gets what he wants. But each success serves to deepen rather than to relieve despair. The real message pivots on Piet Hanema, the book's sturdiest, yet most pathetic character, whose adventures in adultery are reluctant but grow to be well nigh insatiable. "America is like an unloved child smothered in candy," laments the disillusioned Piet, whose faith in his family's church, in the American way, in his own moral standards is gradually slipping away. "God doesn't love us anymore. He loves Russia. He loves Uganda. We're fat and full of pimples and always whining for more candy. We've fallen from grace." He anesthetizes the pain by sleeping, in turn, with a bevy of local ladies. Like John Millington Synge, John Updike is claiming to tell it as it is.

If the playboy were willing to examine his position critically, he might learn, as have many generations of thinkers, that it is more vulnerable than he supposes. Only ignorance of the past can explain the present pleasure-seeker's implicit appeal to a widely discredited theory that all human beings are motivated only by the desire for happiness—nothing else. Diogenes Laertius was one of this theory's earliest proponents; he adduced that all living things, from birth on, crave pleasurable experiences and are at enmity with pain. His contention was that, consciously or unconsciously, man's pursuit of aims

43

like wealth, or power, or virtuous character was only a means to achieving the end—pleasure. This tactic is really an effort to establish what men *ought* to do, by citing what they are already doing. One of the popular devices of playboyism is: "Let's be honest; since everybody is out for his own pleasure anyway, why don't we just say so and get on with it?" Even if it were a fact that men always *do* desire what is good, such a maneuver breaks the rule of logic that we cannot infer directly from what men actually do to what they *ought* to do.

If the definition of pleasure includes such concepts as joy, bliss, fulfillment—all that we ordinarily mean by happiness—then every man is a hedonist. Even when a man goes to the dentist, his motive might be pleasure-seeking, since his willingness to face pain is prompted by a desire for future pleasure. The martyr submits to burning; the parent sacrifices for his child; the ascetic embraces rigors of self-denial—all for the purpose of achieving what, subconsciously or in the long term, promises to bring the highest happiness. But the pleasure principle, if interpreted to mean so much, really means nothing at all. It can transpose an arch-opponent, like Immanuel Kant, into a thoroughgoing playboy, because Kant's answer to the pleasure motive was that God rewards with happiness those who perform duty for duty's sake. If such a sweeping definition of pleasure stands, the thesis of Kant's rebuttal is demonstrated but not denied. The hopes of mankind, embodied in all religion, also verify hedonism insofar as religion invokes the bliss of heaven and the pangs of hell as motivation for morality. If pleasure is understood in this all-inclusive sense, Henry Sidgwick, the British utilitarian, should not be faulted for describing the ethics of Jesus as hedonistic. The Christian, at least, in part, renounces temporal pleasure for the sake of higher happiness in this world and the next.

This doctrine was clearly formulated in Jeremy Bentham's *An Introduction to the Principles of Morals and Legislation:*

"Nature has placed mankind under the governance of two sovereign masters, *pain* and *pleasure*. It is for them alone to point out what we ought to do, as to determine what we shall do. On the one hand, the standard of right and wrong; on the other hand, the chain of causes and effects are fastened to their throne. They govern us in all we do, in all we say, in all we think; every effort we can make to throw off our subjection will serve but to demonstrate and confirm it. In words a man may pretend to abjure their empire; but in reality he will remain subject to it all the while." Volition, in other words, is always determined by the greatest pleasure in prospect.

Consistently followed, the logic of Bentham's words leads, inevitably, to a vicious determinism which, in turn, renders the whole question of ethics meaningless. For, if no one can help pursuing at all times the greatest pleasure in prospect, there is no basis for the moral *ought,* because ought has meaning only if there is a choice between alternative courses of action. If volition is determined by feeling, the efficacy of reason is destroyed, which means that the difference between right and wrong loses all meaning. Both martyr and murderer are propelled by a desire for pleasure and are unable to act in any other way. There is no essential difference between Francis of Assisi and Adolph Eichmann—each sought his own pleasure, albeit in different ways. This theory of human motivation is a denial of freedom—a terrifying conception of life in which there is no escape from fatalism. The playboy is *not* turned loose to do as he pleases, he is absolutely predetermined to do as he must. He may *feel* free to pursue his pleasures, but, if he is intellectually consistent, he is forced to admit that his apparent freedom is an illusion and that he is, as Bentham put it, bound to "a sovereign master" much more tyrannical than the Calvinistic God. If this theory were a true account of the psychology of motivation, it would not ordain the pursuit of pleasure as the supreme system of ethics but would render hedonism, along with all other ethical theories, completely irrelevant.

Only by the most tortured line of logic may all acts of altruism, self-denial, or commitment to duty be accounted for as the pursuit of pleasure in disguise. The writings of Freud are celebrated for detailed treatment of the complexities of human motivation and most contemporary psychologists regard the pleasure-only incentive as a gross oversimplification. Our motives are complex, and in most instances, while desire for pleasant experience may be one of the elements involved, it is seldom the only element. To acknowledge that all men are frequently motivated by pleasure, or even that some men always are, is not to prove that *all* men in *all* their undertakings are pursuing pleasure and nothing else.

When one moves from the field of psychology into the study of ethics, the key verb changes from *is* to *ought;* and the theory that even if men do not always seek their own pleasure they *ought* to do so is *ethical hedonism.* This view of life recommends that the right action at any moment is the one which will lead to the maximum possible pleasure for the agent. Again, the difficulty of deciding what should be meant by pleasure has divided the question into several schools of thought. One thing that can be said with certainty, however, is that the idea of pleasure has seldom meant what it means to the playboy of today. To find a genuine prototype of what is now popularly espoused, we must go all the way back to the ancient Cyrenaic School, which held that the only good for man is the pleasure of the present. Moral duty is fulfilled by following pleasure-seeking instincts, crowding as much physical gratification as possible into each day.

So vulnerable to attack was this view that other classical writers were quick to expose it. Through all subsequent centuries there has never been another important philosophical effort to justify raw hedonism. The Cyrenaics were not the last to demonstrate it, however, for men of every age have been drawn to this brand of playboyism. While it has not been popular in theory, the untrammeled pursuit of pleasure has always been prevalent in practice. While *The Playboy Philosophy* is not new, it is, perhaps, the most influential apology for the untrammeled pursuit of pleasure since the days at Cyrenaic.

The most famous pleasure-seekers of antiquity, and the most misunderstood, were the Epicureans, who inherited and altered greatly the Cyrenaic tradition. To identify Epicureanism with Cyrenaicism is clearly a mistake. "When we maintain that pleasure is the end, we do not mean the pleasures of profligates and those that consist in sensuality," Epicurus explained, "but freedom from pain in the body and from trouble in the mind. For it is not continuous drinking and revelings, nor the satisfactions of lusts, nor the enjoyment of fish or other luxuries of the wealthy table, which produce a pleasant life, but sober reasoning." Profoundly influenced by the Socratic doctrine of prudence, Epicurus advised men to aim for the life of enduring rational happiness rather than for short-term gratification. Epicureanism was so far removed from the notion of sensory stimulation it must be regarded as a serious judgment against today's playboyism, not as an apology for it.

Even in its most ancient manifestations, the standard of *maximum quantity of pleasure* was impossible to maintain. The Epicureans evaluated pleasures qualitatively by distinguishing between so-called higher and lower forms. Centuries later the utilitarian hedonists of the Enlightenment were even more definite in drawing such distinctions, and for that reason, they departed much more definitely from the basic premise of simple pleasure-seeking. Although holding to pleasure as the only good, John Stuart Mill, who led this school at its high point in Britain, during the nineteenth century, stressed that some *kinds* of pleasure are more desirable and valuable than others. Mill concluded that the pleasure criterion must never mean mere quantity, conceding that it is morally better to be a Socrates dissatisfied than a pig satisfied.

While the pleasure principle may be expanded into a complex philosophy cluttered with alternatives, its essential premise has never been proved to be true. Plato was the first to point out that hedonism, regardless of its form, cannot avoid the horns of an irresolvable dilemma: it is either morally unacceptable or inherently inconsistent. If, as in Cyrenaicism, it chooses to abide by the rule that quantity of pleasure is all that counts, it inevitably drifts into an unrelieved sensualism; because the level of sensation must be constantly increased in order to sustain the same level of enjoyment. If, on the other hand, as in Epicureanism and Utilitarianism, it chooses to rate pleasures qualitatively, admitting that some are superior to others, even if less pleasant, it falls into inconsistency and contradicts the logic of its own premises. The very attempt to moderate pleasure-seeking with a qualitative differentiation leads inescapably to the admission of some standard other than pleasure itself.

John Stuart Mill was torn by a fierce dilemma, which illustrates the essential incompatibility between hedonism and humanism: his intellect told him that he ought to be a pleasure-seeker, but his nature implored him to live life like a hero. He sought to solve the dilemma by performing a wedding between the pleasure principle and social reform. "The greatest happiness of the greatest number" became the slogan of his Utilitarian movement which sought the wide distribution of human pleasure and welfare. By becoming a social reformer, Mill could no longer be a hedonist. Unquestionably the influence of Christianity, caused Mill and his colleagues to amend their philosophy with outgoing humanistic devotion, and they ended up with something other than the simple pleasure principle. Despite the glaring inconsistency of his position, Mill, unlike lesser apologists for his faith, never tried to argue that Socrates drank hemlock because it made him happy or that Jesus went to the cross for the pleasure of it.

By holding to their simple definition of quantity of pleasure, however, the Cyrenaics avoided inconsistency only to be impaled on the other horn. They were trapped in an unrelieved sensualism. The Cyrenaics provide the pattern, both in their definition of pleasure and in the definitions' ultimate consequences, for today's pleasure cult.

Observing the tragic mistake of the Cyrenaics, Epicurus warned that the so-called lower pleasures are not only ephemeral in themselves, but are also productive of so great an amount of pain that the prudent man cannot regard them as truly pleasurable. The higher pleasures—health of body and the soul's freedom from disturbance—may be achieved only under the guidance of reason and restraint. The negative side of Epicureanism was developed to such an extent that the ideal life came to be not positive pleasure, but indifference to pain. The consequence of this dilemma is pessimism, which stems from unresolved contradictions. In the name of pleasure, the Epicureans came to advocate severe repression and self-denial. They shielded themselves from abounding pain by withholding themselves from abounding pleasure. Their deepest yearning was for *ataraxia*—tranquility. Coming to the conclusion that the only real peace is the grave, Hegesius wrote *The Privilege to Die;* and the third book of Lucretius climaxes in an eloquent rhapsody on death. Having started with the premise that pleasure is the end of life, they concluded that since life affords as much pain as pleasure, the end of life is impossible of achievement. Many an Epicurean found his pathway to pleasure in the grave.

Many pleasure-seekers in our modern world have been driven to the same desperate conclusion. "There is no remedy for anything in life," Ernest Hemingway wrote in *Death in the Afternoon*. "Death is the sovereign remedy for all our misfortunes." The best information to be gleaned from the human struggle warns that the surest way to miss happiness is to seek it directly. If a person has no sense of meaning in life beyond his own pleasures, even the pleasures themselves soon turn sour. The very rich, or those with great physical beauty, are not necessarily supremely happy; they may be very sad. Often, the most unhappy people are those who, surrounded by every material comfort, lack a sense of inner well-being and who must rush through a hectic schedule of entertainments. Sometimes they learn that pleasure is a hard master, an appetite that grows on what it feeds. It is a physiological fact that a stimulated muscle reflexively demands greater stimulation, and people become enslaved by their passions in much the same way. With each overindulgence, the level of physical and emotional expectation gradually rises so that an increasingly greater thrill is required to satisfy the urge. Eventually, the thrill begins to diminish but the hunger for stimulation is ever present, now stronger than ever. Without finding full satisfaction, the hunger need settles into the monotony of filling and emptying. One begins by seeking pleasures to fill his boredom and ends by being bored with his pleasures. As Shakespeare said, "If all the years were playing holidays, to sport would be as tedious as to work."

The real victims of our pleasure-crazed, affluent society are the young people. Often they get too much too soon. Rarely having to do without, they do not learn to cope with frustrations and they build up a threshold of expectation of immediate satisfaction for all desires. By the time they reach high school, a number are weary of the usual pleasures and are looking for more excitement. Some turn to dope, others to perversion. Rebelling against the inconsistencies of middle-class values, the hippie subculture has decided that the pathway to self-realization is through consuming anything that turns you on; making love however and whenever you want, to whomever you can find that feels good and doesn't hurt anybody; saturating the senses with color and music, light and motion until the mind blows. The increasing use of drugs is an inevitable consequence of having begun on the pathway of seeking ultimate fulfillment through immediate satisfaction. The teen-ager who takes LSD, which its adherents have termed "instant ecstasy," may have learned his lesson from his father. Although his father abstains from this particular vice, he may have taught his son that life should be regarded as a constant round of immediate pleasure. Perhaps every father should see the suicide note written by a North Carolina college student: "I'm tired of being so damned happy!"

Despite the fact that many oversimplify the search for pleasure, ours is a world in which the possibilities for human happiness are great, and there are many genuinely happy people in it. If any common truth emerges from an examination of these happy lives it is that happiness is a by-product rather than a goal.

Some of the happiest people are those who have been so absorbed in some worthy undertaking, or so devoted to a cause, that they have not had time to raise the question of whether they were personally happy. The teacher devoted to his students, the parent preoccupied with the welfare of his child, the craftsman or poet engaged in a work which seems of enduring value—these are the people who may be gloriously happy because they have given themselves to the task at hand, with no ulterior motives. How strikingly such abundant lives contrast with those people, usually of ample wealth and physical charm, who line up at the minister's door or lie down on the psychiatrist's couch to ask why they are not happy.

If you ask the truly happy people if they are happy they are surprised at the question because it has never occurred to them to ask it.

Whatever else is problematic, we may be certain that happiness is lost if it is made the dominant goal of a person's life; yet it may come if it is neglected. The ethical consensus of the ages is decisive at this point.

3.

The Freedom of the Individual

> When one begins with unlimited freedom he ends with unlimited despotism.
>
> Fyodor Dostoyevsky

THE DESIRE for freedom comes closer to summing up what the human enterprise is all about than does any other single idea, and the playboy philosophy centers upon this ancient search. Every ideal that is distorted by playboyism is distorted because of its unrealistic view of freedom. The playboy wants individual freedom to seek his own pleasure, and he wants others to be tolerant so he can be absolutely free. Inherent in this quest is a profound misunderstanding of the nature of the individual and the nature of freedom. His idea of individualism is an apology for selfishness; his idea of freedom distorts liberty into license.

The dignity and worth of the individual is the cornerstone upon which the Western democracies are built. Our basic conviction is that, in the world as we know it, there are but two realities—*persons* and *things*. We believe that the most clear-cut of all divisions in the universe is the line that separates the two. Any one person above that line is worth more than all of the *things* combined below it.

Below the line, elements and objects and animals may be classified according to their group characteristics and, within each group, may be regarded as essentially duplicating examples of the entire species. We do not, as a rule, accord to the things below the line infinite worth. For this reason vivisection and other forms of scientific experimentation are considered ethically acceptable by most people. But, above the line, individual characteristics take precedence over group characteristics so that human vivisection, such as that practiced by Hitler's doctors, is regarded as unconditionally evil. The ethical consensus is that no human being may be used as a guinea pig; persons are infinitely precious, while things are not. Things are of instrumental value and may be *used* as we may need them, but persons are of ultimate worth and are to be *loved* as ends within themselves. It is immoral to reverse these priorities—to love things and to use persons. The essential immorality is to use persons as though they were things, and it is clearly the playboy's intention to make the girl a plaything.

For moral rather than physical reasons every human being must be regarded as uniquely precious. When we say that every individual is a *person* we mean that he is not only a creature who is capable of thought, but also one who is able to think about his thinking; that out of this reflection and a sense of duty he may say "No" to his instinctive appetites; that as a center of value and of valuing he may raise the question of *oughtness* and thereby cultivate a sense of distinction between right and wrong. It is in this moral consideration, not in the biological sphere, that his dignity as a person resides. While no person's fingerprint or footprint is identical with that of any other person, anywhere or at any time, this is not a crucial consideration, since the same may be said for an oak leaf or a snowflake. What is infinitely precious is not the mere biological organism, but the *person* as a unique center of individual desires and aspirations. There is about each person, not only something important, but something which is also inviolable.

The dignity and worth of the individual are being threatened in our time—partly because there are more of us than ever before, many living under conditions of congestion, commotion and speed. But the more serious threat to the individual's dignity arises from ethical confusion. We are losing much of the reverence for the single person and putting our confidence, instead, in high-powered machinery, majority opinion, big budgets and collective bargaining.

Many in our culture derive a sense of security and self-esteem from affiliations and memberships in groups, rather than from an appreciation of their own inherent worth as persons. Such persons are almost certain to know moments of insecurity and low self-esteem. Does the group give value to the individual, or does the individual give value to the group? Is a man important in his own right or because of the union to which he belongs? Or the church? Or the nation of which he is a citizen? This basic question is at stake in the struggle between the hemispheres. Our side of the world, at least in theory, raises the banner of the individual while the other side champions the cause of collective power. Much of the difference is merely rhetorical, however, because the arresting fact is the degree to which the two sides are similar. Labels notwithstanding, we are more like the Russians than we wish to admit; and nowhere is the similarity more apparent than in our haste to concede that human strength lies in organizations and collectives. Frequently, it appears that the most important thing about a man is not the merit and impact of his personality, but the dossier chronicling his numerous organizations.

The mighty currents of history have flowed from persons. The solar theory, which laid a new floor in the house of knowledge, was not the joint research project of the astronomy department at some university; it came, with suffering, from the mind of Copernicus. Plays in which the English language reached its zenith were not the product of a school of sixteenth-century scholars; they issued from the gifted pen of Shakespeare. The link between bacteria and infectious disease was not forged by an abstraction called nineteenth-century France, it was painstakingly developed by crippled researcher Louis Pasteur. Not a committee of scientists, but the brilliant brain of Albert Einstein developed the relativity theory. When General Marshal Ferdinand Foch sought to inspire individual initiative among his French troops during the first world war he exclaimed, "It was not an army that crossed the Alps; it was Hannibal!" And William James, when asked to define spirituality, replied that he could best do so, not with words but with personality; he named Phillips Brooks. Without the Mayo brothers and their clinic, Rochester, Minnesota, would be just another small town.

Our inclination to underestimate the individual was dramatized by H. T. Webster's famous 1909 cartoon, which celebrated the one-hundredth anniversary of Abraham Lincoln's birth. The picture shows two Kentucky frontiersmen pausing to visit on a snow-covered trail; bare trees stand gaunt against leaden winter sky, as one frontiersman asks: "Any news down t' th' village, Ezry?" His friend answers, "Well, Squire Mc-Clean's gone t' Washin'ton t' see Madison swore in, an' ol' Spellman tells me this Bonapart fella has captured most o' Spain. What's new out here, neighbor?" "Nuthin' a-tall, nuthin' a-tall, 'cept for a new baby down t' Tom Lincoln's. Nuthin' ever happens out here."

Real power is always packaged as persons, and it is channeled into the universe through the lives of individuals. If we go looking for it in some colossal undertaking, we may miss it altogether. The essence of Biblical revelation is that when the time arrived for the Creator to reveal Himself in some specific form, He did not choose a monument or a mountain or a star or a set of laws, He chose the medium of human personality.

If ever a culture hungered for a return to the doctrine of

individualism, ours does, which is one of the main reasons the playboy philosophy has created such excitement. Exploding populations compressed into huge, machine-ruled cities are delighted to hear someone say, "What we believe in, first and foremost, is the individual—and his right to be an individual." Is it surprising then that Hugh Hefner, who makes this statement in all earnestness, should be regarded as something of a prophet crying out in the asphalt wilderness? "Our view of the world is predicated upon the paramountcy of the individual," he writes, "and each person's inherent individuality." Is it any wonder the college generation of the 1960's, carrying signs reading, "I am a human being; please do not fold, spindle, or mutilate me," responds to this kind of message? Nothing about present-day pleasure-seeking appeals more directly to our computerized culture than this refreshing emphasis upon the importance of the individual.

Unquestionably, Mr. Hefner is telling much that is true, which explains his popular success. But many of history's worst evils have been perpetrated upon mankind in the name of rugged individualism. Although each man is different from all other men, it is also true that no man is an island, entire unto himself. Men must live in community with one another and to talk of individual freedom without talking of the society which makes it possible is to talk nonsense. The fault of the current fad is not that it says too much on this question, but that *what* it says twists the fundamental meaning of the doctrine.

During the Enlightenment one widely-held view was that the interests of society could best be served by programs that encouraged each individual to pursue his own private happiness without conscious regard for the public good. John Locke's pupil, The Earl of Shaftesbury, advanced this position with great success in his *Inquiry Concerning Virtue and Merit*. Shortly thereafter, the *laissez-faire* economics of Adam Smith added weight to the conviction that so-called enlightened self-interest was sufficient for the social good. Within this climate, Bentham and Mill, holding pleasure to be the only possible motive for human action, contended that the wise society should legislate so as to allow each man to seek his own personal pleasure. Selfishness was seen, not as a moral problem, but as a legislative one, evil only if unintelligently directed. The surest way to promote the greatest happiness of the greatest number was to encourage each individual to pursue intelligently his own private happiness. This view was exported to emerging America where religious and commercial values soon became so interwoven that success in business was regarded as a sign of divine favor, a fulfillment of God's intentions. Whatever a man wanted he could have—wealth, women, power—provided he was strong enough to go out and get them.

The best contemporary example of the distortion of individualism may be drawn from the objectivist ethic of Ayn Rand. Following in the Hobbes tradition, Miss Rand refuses to deify the pleasure principle but nonetheless provides aid and comfort to the hedonists because of her forceful defense of the privatist ethic. John Gault, hero of her best-selling *Atlas Shrugged,* summarized the objectivist ethic: "I swear—by my life and by my love of it—that I will never live for the sake of another man, nor ask another man to live for my own." Miss Rand thinks that no idea is more pernicious than that of denying oneself for the benefit of others, which explains why she has been praised by Hugh Hefner. In *Playboy Interviews* Miss Rand summarized her position: "Man exists for his own sake, the pursuit of his own happiness is his highest moral purpose, that he must not sacrifice himself to others nor sacrifice others to himself.

Hefner's playboyism and Rand's egoism are two sides of the same coin—nineteenth-century rugged individualism with a twentieth-century gloss. Both are cultural liberals, but socio-economic reactionaries who defend *laissez-faire* capitalism. Their philosophy is an apology for aggrandizement of the self, with all of the accompanying disorders of arrogance, exaggerated self-importance, and unrealistic self-expectation. What is worse, this perverted individualism is a withdrawal from society which ends up disdaining or exploiting other individuals. One example is the tycoons of nineteenth-century America who fulfilled their own rapacious ambitions, sometimes at the expense of impoverished immigrant labor and of our country's natural resources. This view of life fails to acknowledge that, in our kind of world, men are necessarily interdependent. Miss Rand even entitled one of her polemic books *The Virtue of Selfishness*, and both she and Hefner end up implying that man's best protection against society is to remain outside it.

As always, the playboy has a makeshift maxim at hand to buttress his philosophy of selfmanship:

> *This above all: to thine own self be true,*
> *And it must follow, as the night the day,*
> *Thou canst not then be false to any man.*
> —*Hamlet*, William Shakespeare

The assumption is that if each isolated individual is sufficiently self-seeking and true to his urge, a better society will somehow result. Unfortunately, as is true with virtually all of his Biblical quotations, Hefner snatches this line out of context and fails to notice that Shakespeare put these words into the mouth of the scheming Polonius to reveal how brazen human selfishness can become. The popular philosophy is a travesty of man, an exaggeration of a caricature, which can provide justification for every atrocity. Hitler, after all, never failed to be true to his demonic self. Is there any crime that could not be committed as readily for some individual's self as well as against it? For those who suspect this analysis is too severe, John Cowper's popular book *In Defense of Sensuality*, provides convincing evidence. "If a person has found the secret of a thrilling life of happiness, why should he bother with other people?" asks Cowper. "His only wish concerning them is that they should take themselves off and leave him alone."

Such complete autonomy is, of course, impossible. Ever since the great days in ancient Greece we have known that no individual can be complete master of himself and his fate, cut free from all restraints and ties, a free-soaring bird. Man's social nature is such that true individuality cannot develop except in community. In *Values in a Universe of Chance*, one of America's most original philosophers, Charles S. Pierce, wrote: "We know that man is not whole so long as he is single, that he is essentially a possible member of society. Especially, one man's experience is nothing if it stands alone." And Gabriel Marcel points out that we do not know ourselves first and then postulate others by analogy, but that we are aware of the existence of others before we are aware of our own existence. The human infant is born utterly dependent upon his parents and, for the first few years of his life, he evolves deeply rooted social habits in communication with those who care for him. The chronology of personal awareness is not from self to others, but rather from others to self. Man is social before he is individual because his social character is fixed in his biological nature. All in life that makes us most human involves interaction with other humans. As Josiah Royce once said, a person's life means nothing, either theoretically or practically, unless he is a member of a community. If some great catastrophe should destroy all human beings on earth except one, virtually all human wisdom and ethical considerations would be rendered wholly irrelevant to the lone survivor.

The pleasure paradox, the idea that happiness must be forfeited when it becomes the consuming passion of a person's life, does not stand alone; it is part of the accumulated ethical wisdom that concern for self poisons all of life and is ultimately self-defeating. Modern psychology has concurred that in order for the personality to be healthy it must be extroverted rather than introverted, directed outside rather than inside the self. The object of supreme devotion must be something other than one's own pleasure, or wealth, or reputation. Moral salvation lies in having objectives beyond oneself, in pursuit of which one may forget oneself. These must be objectives which bring integration and wholeness to life without making personal integration and innerwholeness themselves the goal. Happiness is not found in the pursuit of happiness, nor holiness in the pursuit of holiness; both are by-products of the pursuit of something else beyond self that is really worth pursuing and in the pursuit of which a man may safely forget himself. There appears to be something in man's nature that is in harmony with the moral law that states it is fitting to suffer for another's pleasure. It is analogous with the stalk of wheat dying to produce fruit or with the suffering of a mother during childbearing.

No serious thinker ever claims that the individual should be unconcerned about himself, for it is impossible to live well without self-esteem. Much as we may be ashamed of our weaknesses, we must, if we are to achieve human dignity, work out some system by which self-approbation is possible. The Biblical insight that we ought to love our neighbors as we love ourselves, was an amazing anticipation of modern psychology's discovery that it is the man who hates himself who can never really love any of his neighbors. As Aristotle recognized, every individual must establish some kind of relationship with himself and this relationship, of himself to himself, forms the basis for his attitude toward all other individuals.

The man who fails to establish a friendly relationship with himself, and who does not accept and esteem his own being as a person, cannot relate himself in a personal and friendly manner to others. It is an axiom in psychiatry that self-love is the indispensable requisite for all human love, because in order to say, "I love you," one must first be capable of saying the "I." Self-respect, accordingly, is not evil, but is the necessary precondition for both individuality and communality.

What is the distinction between *self-love* and sheer selfishness? Is it a question of extent or degree—a point at which what is a virtue as long as it remains small, turns suddenly into a vice because it grows large? Is self-love valid only in moderation—a little being essential, more being shameful? While this may be a common view, it is a false approach, because self-esteem is a virtue, just as honesty or cleanliness are virtues, and therefore the more of it one develops the better. We are on the road to wisdom when we know that the man who loves himself least can least love his neighbor, while the man who loves himself most is capable of greatest love of his neighbor. We must start from the opposite direction and say that self-love differs from selfishness, not in degree, but in *kind*. They are separate conceptions altogether; without regard to quantity, the one is always right, while the other is always wrong. *What distinguishes them is the view each takes toward others.* Self-love is a wholesome acceptance that releases the individual from personal preoccupation so he may relate himself to the needs and interests of others. Selfishness, on the other hand, is *self-centeredness*, an exclusive devotion to, and concern for, one's own interests and desires.

The fundamental motion of self-love is expansion, while that of selfishness is contraction. Self-love reaches outward toward others; selfishness shrivels ever inward toward itself. The self-respecting father does not resent the victories and accomplishments of his son; he shares them as though they were his own, because the life of the father has expanded to include the life of the son. Because the capacity for human expansion is limitless and certainly great enough to include them all, it makes no difference whether the sons are one or many. When there is no blood relationship the problem of expanding to include the life of another is greater, but the undertaking is not impossible, as we observe daily. The teacher receives joy from the fruitfulness of the students because they become *his* students. The high challenge of life is to make peace with ourselves so that we may extend our life outward to envelop all others who come into it. The person who accepts himself is released to give himself to others; the man who is so unsure of his own worth that he must constantly look inward comes to know the tragedy of living only for himself. If he becomes sufficiently enslaved, he may discover that his life has shriveled until it is only large enough to encircle his psycho-physical appetites and urges.

The fallacy in the playboy's value system is not his emphasis upon pleasure, but his emphasis upon himself. The playboy's idea of individualism stresses desires gratified; the more realistic view emphasizes the capacity to take an interest in another. There is nothing inherently unworthy about any of the sensual activities the playboy has in his lexicon; what is unworthy is concern for self with little or no reference to others.

The relationship of the individual and society is always one of the most controversial and complex questions, but those who encourage the idea of the isolated individual are clearly wrong in any age. Because the social problems of our society are so great, any person who presumes to escape by being free from the influence of others has failed to understand, in an absurd fashion. Sometimes the absurdity is tragic: A young woman attacked and throttled to death, while dozens of people look on, each unwilling or afraid to become involved by telephoning the police from the security of his apartment! A man robbed and beaten on a subway train, while fellow riders remain uninvolved. Such incidents are now quite commonly reported, and, as we read our daily papers, we become aware that many of the onlookers are respectable, friendly folk, who share the sophisticated outlook for which our large cities are so celebrated.

Because of the circumstances of our history, many Americans have come to feel that freedom involves the exclusive connotation of emancipation, of freedom *from* something. Our heritage includes the struggles to be free from a king, from an ecclesiastical hierarchy, and from foreign influence. Our Constitution is based upon what we call freedom's inalienable rights, and one of the sacred documents that attends it is called the Bill of Rights. Unfortunately, in this struggle to overcome every form of oppression and to create a truly free society, we have drifted into a mood in which we are so preoccupied with freedom's rights we give little attention to freedom's duties and responsibilities. Does anyone demonstrate because he feels deprived of freedom's duties?

Ever since our republic won its independence, the cry has been, "Give me more freedom." This cry is valid when it is directed toward tyranny and injustice, but sometimes the freedom we claim is an immunity from all restraint, from any real hardship, from discipline and from sacrifice. There is loose in the land the notion that freedom means the inalienable right of every man to do as he pleases, when or where he pleases. Many of our contemporaries think of freedom, in the sense of the removal of all inhibitions on personal action, as intrinsically unlimited. As a result, we are developing a cast of mind in which children defy parents, students scoff at educational authority, thugs of all kinds flaunt their freedom in increasingly ineffective courts and workers at all levels tend to keep both eyes on the clock with primary concern for what they can get and little interest in what they can give. Every kind of silly, subversive, lewd thing imaginable seeks to be justified by the slogan, "Well, it's a free country isn't it?"

It is important to remember that a government does not give freedom to individuals, but that individuals who become free endow the government with freedom. Since government is a neutral force, its character is determined by the quality of the people who comprise it and it may give people only that which it derives from them. In the beginning, the government is always at the mercy of the people. But if persons shift the responsibility for achieving freedom from themselves to the government they must prepare to live at the mercy of the government. When the voters find that they can grant themselves a cheap, unlimited freedom by empowering the government to give it to them, they must eventually reap the harvest of servitude. Bondage is the reward of believing that the fountainhead of freedom is external rather than internal.

The worst aspect of this popular misconception of freedom is that it is purely negative and focuses primarily on what the individual is *free from* rather than upon what he is *free for*. Personal liberty does not mean that every man is cut loose to do whatever he chooses, but that every man is free so that he may choose to do what he ought. However unpopular it may be to challenge the entrenched position that freedom is everybody's natural right, the time has come to do it, and to say plainly that freedom is not a gift, it is an achievement. It must be earned and will belong *only* to those men and women who are prepared to pay the price.

If we were as willing to learn from our heritage as we have been willing to be victimized by it, we would see that freedom is never free. On every page of American history is moving evidence, and the price has never been so high as it has been during our own very recent past. We must never forget that once there lived a man named Adolf Hitler. We may differ in our opinions regarding the conflict in Southeast Asia, but all honorable men everywhere know that a generation ago there was a madman who had to be stopped, regardless of the cost. And we were stirred when former President John F. Kennedy, in his inaugural address, committed us to continue the payments, no matter how great. "Let every nation know, whether it wishes us ill or well," he said, "that we shall pay any price, bear any burden, meet any hardship, support any friend, oppose any foe to assure the survival and success of liberty." When the new president prophetically added, "This much we pledge and more," he did not know that the "more" would prove to be so much, but he surely knew that freedom is expensive and more precious than life itself. There is cause for alarm when men forget that their freedom has been achieved at the price of heroic sacrifice and that their rights are founded upon their duties.

President Kennedy's shocking assassination serves as a solemn reminder that personal freedom is a paradox: Men ought to be free from tyranny, but absolute freedom produces essential tyranny, which is a risk free men must always be prepared to take. In a sense, human liberty has never been more sweet than in this present hour. Never have men been granted greater freedom to think, to read whatever they please, to speak out, to organize, to question authority—political, religious, or cultural—to write, to stage, to film what even a scant few years ago would have been impermissible. Never has police authority been more scrutinized, never have defendants been so surrounded with legal protections.

But it is always the business of freedom to be dangerous. Its outcome cannot be rigged in advance, for freedom must hazard its future on a faith that cannot guarantee tomorrow. Of course, the free society is shaken and shamed when its executive leader is gunned down in the streets, but that we live in a country where such an event is possible is not only one of the hazards of liberty, but the very glory of the free society. While our enemies may gloat self-righteously, it is the dubious distinction of the Communist philosophy that ordinary men are restricted within a system that precludes such a possibility. Though freedom is a risk, the only alternative is unthinkable.

What should concern us is that President Kennedy's death was not an isolated event, it was but the first in a horrifying sixty-month succession of major political assassinations. Because of our freedoms, never before could it have been so easy for a boy, born in an Arab land on the other side of the globe, to flee his oppressed land and be welcomed into the land of the free; to come and to go openly, enjoying all of the benefits of liberty; to secure a deadly weapon, without fear of molestation; and, with incredible ease, to point it at a United States Senator and pull the trigger eight times. We do not subscribe to the sweeping generalization that senseless acts of a handful implicate an entire nation, but the epidemic of lawlessness is sufficiently widespread to be cause for alarm. Alarm shared by Dwight D. Eisenhower, who closed his two terms in the White House by appointing a special commission to investigate our national purpose; and, by Lyndon B. Johnson, who, near the end of his tenure, appointed a special commission to examine what he called "the phenomena of violence and assassination in America." An administration that began by dreaming of a great society ended in a nightmare of the violent society.

We have clamored for total personal freedom, but now we must face a bleak and chilly truth: Having flung off one restraint after another, we have not learned how to restrain ourselves. We are free in the same sense that a ship is free when it has lost both compass and rudder. We must find our course again, and the way to begin is to ask: To what extent does our *lostness* stem from a distorted concept of freedom that leaves us free to be soft, free to be selfish, free to be ignoble?

What is necessary, for the sake of survival itself, as well as for the sake of the moral life, is a more realistic understanding of the terms of genuine freedom. Freedom is something to be earned, and individual responsibility—discipline at the personal level—is always the price of freedom at the corporate level. Without restraint in the human spirit, the free way of life leads, through self-indulgence and disorder, to the destruction of freedom itself.

Absolute freedom is impossible for any society because society is comprised of individuals and no individual can ever be absolutely free. It is self-destructive for a man to believe that he has the natural right to do as he pleases. He will come to know that the path of supposed freedom leads into bondage, while the very restraint he has defied could have led toward freedom.

Millions who have started out to be set loose have come to loose ends. Parents who indulge their son's every whim so he will be happy and consequently feel love for them, would be wise to prepare for the indolence, self-importance, and irresponsibility that may result. And the quarter-million girls each year who use their freedom for out-of-wedlock pregnancies are discovering how free it really is. Ask the husband who dishonors his marriage vows so he can be uninhibited if the new relationship is any less restricting. Ask the alcoholic who demonstrates his self-determination by reaching for another glass if he is free when he is unable to resist reaching. Ask the generation of flower children who purport to replace the culture of rot and payola with their psychedelic order of pot and peyote if the consequent liberty is really rewarding. Many have dropped out of society to pursue the ultimate in freedom, but, in abandoning themselves to the lower nature, they have entered the essential slavery. A sixfold increase in venereal disease, an increasing demand for welfare handouts, vacuous stares hidden behind dark glasses—these are not convincing testimonials to emancipation, they reveal enslavement, instead. "No man is free," wrote Seneca, "when he is a slave to his flesh." We take an important step forward when we realize that, like it or not, we are going to be governed by something.

Only when individual men are free, because they are disciplined, can the society of men be free. Anglo-Irish statesman Edmund Burke said, "Men are qualified for civil liberties in exact proportion to their disposition to put moral chains upon their own appetites. Society cannot exist unless a controlling power upon will and appetite be placed somewhere, and the less of it there is within, the more there must be without. It is ordained in the eternal constitution of things that men of intemperate minds cannot be free. Their passions forge their fetters." The important idea in Burke's words is that if we are unwilling to control our own lives through self-discipline, we shall one day, and perhaps gladly so, be controlled by the stern discipline of totalitarianism. The point made by such books as Eric Fromm's *Escape from Freedom* and Eric Hoffer's *The True Believer* is that finally there comes a time of anarchic individualism in which people yearn for stern efficiency and the order of domination. One of the greatest dangers of cheap personal freedom is that, as Plato said in his *Republic,* it prepares the ground for tyranny.

The abuse of freedom in one extreme leads directly to the absence of freedom in the opposite extreme. Students at Columbia University, who commandeered President Graydon Kirk's office and sacked it so thoroughly that all that remained of his personal effects was an ash tray, should not have been shocked when paddy wagons came to meet brute force with force. What makes campus rioters think they can take things forcibly into their own hands without force, in the form of troops or legislature, coming onto the campus?

Freedom is social, and it is always limited by the fact that we must live together on this planet. If the freedom of each man to pursue purely private pleasure is taken as the ethical *norm,* and the gratification of any and all personal *desire* is taken as the ethical *goal,* men will be left with no choice but to fear, despise and hate one another, because their private pleasures and desires will necessarily clash. One man's desire to produce goods and another man's desire to steal them will have equal ethical validity; one man's desire to be free will have no more ethical claim than another man's desire to enslave him; one man's desire to fulfill his sexual urge in liaison with his neighbor's wife will be as ethically valid as her husband's desire to preserve the sanctity of his home. All of which means that the idea of each man being free to pursue his own private happiness by fulfilling his every desire, far from being an absolute ethical right, is an invitation to ethical anarchy. The deepest error of the modern pleasure cult lies in the implicit premise that freedom gives one man the right to pursue his own pleasure, regardless of the community.

There are two dangers that must be avoided: One is the glorification of society in order to abuse the individual; the other is to glorify the individual at the expense of the common good. We must resist the collective trends in modern life that jeopardize the individual's integrity as a free and morally responsible being; but, at the same time, we must encourage every individual to establish a meaningful relationship with a larger context of purposes.

Truly creative individualists do not spend valuable energy in an effort to create the image of being different. Such opposites, and occasional opponents, as Churchill and Gandhi were at one in the common search for justice and truth, yet how differently were the dramas each played out. Individ-

70

ualism is not something to be consciously talked about, nor is it something to preen one's self on. It issues naturally from the uniqueness of each person. Out of this will emerge our inevitable interaction with other individuals. The personality easily suited to the ways of social intercourse will find that the rewards are even more immediate. And the personality tempted to retreat and claim autonomy from people will be hoist by his own petard; for he, too, is a citizen in the community of men, and will, if he is himself, fall victim to the nectar of brotherhood.

The ideal, then, is never rugged individualism, but a societal system for the sake of the individuals who go to make up the society. Something beyond mere individualism must be achieved if the precious values of individualism are to be maintained. While we must reject the totalitarian notion that man's highest fulfillment is to become a member of the faceless mass, we must reject with equal decisiveness the naïve idea of absolute personal autonomy. The interests of the individual and the interests of society are not incompatible, but they are dual values that must be held together, and held in constant tension. If, by neglect of individuals, glorification of society creates tyranny, glorification of the individual, by neglect of the ordered system, becomes anarchy. Bentham put the ideal cogently: "The interest of the community then is what?—the sum of the interests of the several members who compose it."

The group is never valuable unless it upholds the freedom of the individual. The individual never comes to fulfillment except in the fellowship of the group.

4.

The Gift of Sex

Love does not consist in gazing at each other but in looking outward together in the same direction.

Antoine de Saint Exupery

THE CHIEF way in which the moral revolution has been distorted in our generation is by the exploitation of sex. Human beings, like all animals, participate in sexual experience, yet they differ radically from all other creatures in the way in which they have become self-conscious about the experience. Like other creatures, humans enjoy intercourse but, unlike other creatures, they think about it! If this fact were untrue, those who have a commercial stake in promoting sexual interest would not have a hearing.

Day after day people, especially our young people, are bombarded with stimulation of desires that require no stimulation. Combined efforts of motion pictures, magazine advertisements and television commercials amount to an avalanche of propaganda. Our young people are exposed to an exaggerated view of sex from the time they can first hear and see. But there are optimistic signs that many young people are too sophisticated to fall for this line. There seems to be a growing suspicion that a whole establishment of pitchmen and preachers has made sex a biological idol—much more important than it really is. An increasing number of young people feel that when sex becomes the master of life it takes time and energy away from more important things, such as improving the world. A verse in one of the Berkeley free speech songs goes:

> *Sleeping on the lawn*
> *In a double sleeping bag*
> *Doesn't get things done.*

Sex is not a biological appendage; it is an aspect of human existence by which every man, through his attitudes and actions, reveals something of his deepest convictions about life itself. A thorough study of any society, ancient or modern, must always include careful information about its sexual practices, for nothing drives more quickly to the heart of a people's values or provides a surer index into their total view of life. When we discover what men regard as right and wrong in sexual ethics we learn what they believe about much else. Most important of all, it is in the relationships of sex that men mirror their basic beliefs concerning their own nature, their origin and dignity as men.

A distorted Christianity must bear at least some of the blame for the sexual disorders of our society. Much of the history of Christianity reveals negative reaction to everything venereal, a reaction that touches every degree of intensity from apathy to violent revulsion. The Bible itself, however, cannot honestly be regarded as the source of such negativity since, from its opening pages, the sexual relationships between men and women are pictured in a highly positive manner. The author of Genesis minces no words. "The man and his wife were both naked, and were not ashamed." The Old Testament, in such books as the Song of Solomon, celebrates the sexual embrace of lovers in a majestic manner. In the New Testament this positive treatment is continued; there is nothing in the teachings of Jesus to suggest that sexual desire or pleasure is bad. The writings of Paul, although sometimes cited as support for the antisexualism which emerged, when read in total context, actually serve to enhance the goodness of sex. Even Paul, who thought a single life better than a married one, found in marriage the mystical analogy for Christ's union with the church. Furthermore, it was Paul who detailed the conjugal rights and duties of husbands and wives, warning that neither should be deprived the pleasures of sexual intercourse. People who take the Bible seriously are the last to be embarrassed by sex.

Every sound philosophy must include some elements of psycho-physical dualism because it is the obvious record of experience that some attributes refer to thought while others refer to bodies. But there are many kinds of dualism; some are beneficent, others are damaging. One of the most damaging is the one that teaches that the contrast between spirit and body is essentially a moral contrast, the bodily desires being evil. This idea was absorbed into Christian thought from Greek mysticism, which viewed man as a soul chained to and conquered by an evil body. The separation was no simple conflict between will and desire, but an essential fragmentation of being. Man was not one, but two; while his soul could respond to good, his body was inescapably inclined to evil. In fairness to the Greeks, it should be said that their dualism did not associate the flesh with sexual evil only, it considered the fleshly predicament as the door that invites all evil. This fatal distinction embedded itself in the whole attitude of the church, until, for some, fleshly evil was narrowed down to mean sexual sins exclusively.

Sometimes, the isolation of sex from the larger range of moral questions has created such a preoccupation with sexual sins that the church has failed to speak out against other evils. Why is it that the phrase "morals charge" immediately implies sexual deviation, rather than unfair business practices or exploitation of labor? Why is it that when we speak of "living in sin" we never mean living in prejudice or practicing racial discrimination? Because of the inordinate concentration upon sexual morality, the righteous indignation of the church has often been wasted on irrelevant matters, while great moral issues have gone begging.

At no point does the message of Jesus contrast more strikingly with what some Christians through the ages have preached and practiced than the area of sex. St. Augustine by the end of the fourth century, had developed the doctrine of original sin in such a manner as virtually to equate it with sexual pleasure. Soon the conviction was firmly entrenched that, inside or outside of marriage, an act of intercourse propelled by desire and consumated for pleasure is always wrong. Perpetual virginity thus came to be considered the highest good and absolute celibacy was required by all who would take churchly vows. Marriage was permitted as a concession to the weak but, even within marriage, intercourse was looked upon as a necessary evil legitimate only for the propagation of the race. Augustine regarded marriage as a kind of confessional arrangement, a sacrificial means of forgiveness for the sin involved in the pleasure of coitus; and Aquinas, arguing that wedlock with intercourse is really more holy, quoted with approval the saying of philosopher Xystus: "He who loves his own wife too ardently is an adulterer."

The Protestant Reformation, which one might assume to have fostered a return to a more liberal stance, brought little change in attitudes toward sex except that it introduced the concept of a married clergy. Though Martin Luther repudiated the double standard, which set virginity above marriage as a state of grace, he continued to regard marital intercourse as a necessary evil, dogmatizing that it was impossible to pray in the marriage bed. Until 1928 the wedding service described marriage as "a remedy against sin, and to avoid fornication;

75

that such persons as have not the gift of continency might marry, and keep themselves undefiled members of Christ's body." Not until 1928 were contraceptives, used within marriage, legalized so far as members of the Angelican communion were concerned.

When those in the Protestant tradition have not been blaming the Catholics they have been charging the Puritans with the whole antisexual history. Though it is fashionable these days to castigate the Puritans, prudery did not begin with, nor find its most excessive manifestations in that movement. To charge the Puritans with all of the qualities found under the popular heading "puritanical" is far from historically accurate. David Bell argues convincingly that the legend of puritanical beliefs has arisen out of mistaken identification of the Protestant ethic with that code. So-called puritanism is actually the product of influences developed much later in American history and would be more accurately attributable to other causes. The Puritans were, of course, highly restrictive and they held an unfortunate view of human depravity, but they should be commended for being consistent and evenhanded in sexual practices, in that they rejected the male-female double standard and urged chastity for both. Those who use the Puritans as a handy instrument of derision to dismiss any effort at moral discipline succeed only in revealing their own superficial understanding.

Modern Roman Catholics also should not be held accountable for medieval ideas. They are caught by their heritage in an awkward trap which one of their theologians has termed "the Pope's predicament of the pill." This predicament has been heightened by Pope Paul's controversial 1968 encyclical against the use of birth control devices within marriage. Millions of Catholics now find themselves actively resisting the voice of ecclesiastical authority. We may be thankful that Catholic clergymen themselves are in the vanguard of world opinion insisting upon a reversal of the recent legislation. But, until it forthrightly affirms the legitimate place of sexual pleasure as a unitive embrace, without regard to procreation, the church will continue to encourage the ancient idea that there is something inherently evil about the sex act itself. And mere endorsement of the rhythm method is no such affirmation. The most debilitating thing about the rhythm method is not that it imposes an abnormal limitation upon the expression of marital love, but that it undergirds the false idea that sex is a biological appetite that can be scheduled—like eating or sleeping. If we hold to the principle that the only purpose of intercourse is procreation and carry this principle to its logical consequence, we cannot avoid the grotesque conclusion that all intercourse after menopause is illicit.

Serious anthropological confusion lies at the root of all this antisexualism. Whenever there is confusion about the nature of man there will always be confusion about much else. Religious antisexualism emerges from a sadly limited definition of man, a view that divorces sexuality from his total being. Such a view segregates sex and translates it into a limited set of actions that may be regulated by law, or discarded with impunity.

Since sex is the very source of new lives we may properly expect it to reveal something about the meaning of life. If it has no meaning beyond the merely biological, then it has no ultimate meaning at all, and neither does the life it initiates. We may never be able to prove that meaning absolutely, but we shall continue to hope that sex reveals something profound and elevating about the nature of man. If it does not, the alternative is grim indeed.

During this century, the science of psychology has added to our knowledge of human sexuality, enabling us to see that we are indelibly sexual beings, not people with or without sex, as we may choose. As children, long before puberty, we are drawn into the experience of sex and even the person who remains a virgin throughout his lifetime is not sexless for that reason. Sex is not essentially something man does, but something he is; sex does not designate a simple function, it relates to the totality of existence. The biological side of sex cannot be isolated and viewed as autonomous because it is but one aspect of the whole, indivisible man. Sexual intercourse is not merely one physical act among many; it is, instead, an act that engages and expresses the entire personality in such a way as to provide insight into the nature of man.

Long before Sigmund Freud, the author of Genesis understood and hinted at the profound relationship between sexuality and the nature of man. "God created man, in the likeness of God made he him; male and female created he them, and blessed them, and called their name Adam, in the day when they were created" (Genesis 5:1, 2 ASV). Those who have overlooked this creation account in the fifth chapter of Genesis, and concentrated on the account in the earlier chapters, will be surprised to see that, at the outset, Adam was not the name of the man and Eve the name of the woman; the word "Adam"—the Hebrew term meaning mankind—designated both man and woman. In other words, "Adam" was not a separate person but a whole person of which male and female soon became the relational poles. The early rabbis interpreted the creation story as being God's way of resolving the original oneness of "Adam" into sexual components. Though male and female were seen as receiving individual existence, both acknowledged immediately their common origin, "bone of my bone and flesh of my flesh."

In this ancient and highly sophisticated account of man's beginnings, human sexual differentiation is not pictured, as with the lower species, only for the purpose of populating the earth, nor as the biological appendage for providing pleasure. The sexual distinction is seen as existing essentially in the

78

nature of man, which suggests that manhood means more than maleness and womanhood more than femaleness. The significance of manhood and womanhood resides, not in what each is unto itself, but in what each can become along with the other. As radically different as they are, yet perfectly complementary, man and woman hunger innately to immerse their separate, prior selves into one complete self. Each yearns to know the other fully, to experience the mutual completeness possible only through communion with the other. By "cleaving" together, the Hebrew term that suggests sexual union in the creation story, they become one flesh; thus achieving a semblance of the fundamental unity of the original "Adam." The longing to be complete through contact and communication with another human being is made possible through the majestic gift of sexual intercourse.

The contemporary pleasure cult is but an inverted form of classic antisexualism. It is obvious that the ordinary playboy has a Puritanical preoccupation with the subject of sex. The new emancipation, so widely discussed for the past fifty years, has resulted, paradoxically, in encouraging the limited view of sex. Our attention has been called away from the evil of the act to the good of the act; but we continue to think of it as an *act*, a physiological function separated from the total being of man. The playboy philosophy perpetuates the synthetic view of man, in which sex is reduced to his genital parts. The fallacy of such a view is that it makes too little of sex, not too much, for it isolates what was meant to pervade and makes small what was intended to be large. Thus the popular philosophy falls into the same fallacy as that of the religious heritage it affects to despise.

When sex is segregated to the biological side of man's nature, it is separated from man's total being, and intercourse is reduced to a mere function. It is extremely important to distinguish clearly between *function* and *being*. *Being* signifies the very ground of man's existence as a person of infinite value, with ultimate dignity as an end in himself. A *function* is but an exercise of being, an activity by which man steps out of himself in order to perform some deed without ultimate significance. The leaders of abnormal psychology are now very much aware that man's being cannot be isolated from his functions without pathological results. We have learned, for instance, that the most rewarding occupations are those in which being and function are closely related. The man who stands at an assembly line screwing the same kind of bolt into scores of identical fenders day after day may perform the labor function in a purely mechanical fashion because his work is not meaningfully related to his being. The craftsman or poet, on the other hand, is capable of producing gloriously and joyously, because he becomes personally involved in his work. A sense of security and significance results when men are given an opportunity to be creative with their hands or with their minds.

It is essentially immoral to regard a person as the bearer of a function—a mere functionary—for then personhood is impugned at the deepest level. Persons are thereby mechanized because, insofar as they are capable of performing a required function, they became interchangeable at will. The economic materialism of Engels and Marx tends to make men the impersonal representatives of the labor force. Under such a system, when a man is no longer capable of performing the functions of labor he is no longer of value. Biological materialism, such as that advocated by Hitler, views man as the impersonal bearer of propagational apparatus, the raw material for population politics. All materialistic philosophies regard sex as a function and view marriage as merely instrumental. Societies that have reflected this view always favor easy divorce, when one of the partners is found to be incapable of performing the procreative function. Our own culture, which is decisively materialistic in practice, holds that partners should not be bound when they decide that they are incompatible—a weasel word, which often means one partner does not perform the physical function to the full satisfaction of the other. Such a view of marriage does not regard the husband and wife as bound together in a relationship of being, but as involved in a functional liaison.

The evidence of antiquity and the findings of modern psychology concur in the conclusion that sexual intercourse is not one act among many; it is an act without comparison, a possibility for achieving and expressing human fulfillment unique unto itself. Thus, the abuse of sexuality is a serious assault upon man's very nature. Sexual intercourse involves more than the body; it involves the whole person, or, more accurately, two whole persons. Whether they give themselves wholly to one another is one thing, but that they are *wholly* involved is beyond doubt. No act of sexual union may ever be regarded as recreational or as one person's private business, for someone else is always profoundly implicated, and the participants will never again be the same toward one another as they were before coming together. Once done, the experience can never be undone, and its effect, though imperceptible, is indelible. If they are husband and wife the embrace should be both source and symbol of the common life they are building together. But if they are not husband and wife, the sexual act is of such inherent significance that its unitive power is frustrated. Intercourse without obligation depersonalizes the parties involved, uniting them in an act of mutual exploitation. It is not because it is temporary, but because, in a sense, casual sex always involves permanent consequences, that it is intrinsically wrong. The playboy creed encourages fornication without involvement.

The words of the famous creed are: "Anything in sex is OK as long as no one gets hurt." This proviso seems adequate to

81

many otherwise thoughtful people, because they do not examine carefully the meaning of "hurt." Given our human finitude, we do not always know who is hurt, for life is such an intricate maze that acts which seem trivial at the moment may bring injury years later. The consequences of human conduct are so far-reaching that no moral decision is ever an isolated one. There are many ways in which one can be hurt, in addition to obvious physical ones.

Sometimes the "hurt" is felt by the whole society, for the community consequences of sexual intimacy are far-reaching for both good and ill. The union of Abraham Lincoln's parents was a profoundly social act as was that of the parents of Adolf Hitler. Though the act itself is initiated by two private individuals, the consequences are seldom restricted to them. Despite all of the knowledge and discussion of birth control, the number of illegitimate births among teen-agers doubled between 1940 and 1964, and, in the same period, nearly quadrupled for the twenty to twenty-five age group. Perhaps it is because fear of pregnancy is no longer considered a deterrent that one out of every five girls who has intercourse before marriage becomes pregnant, which leads to hasty marriage or abortion. How can a couple build a marriage when they must walk down the aisle to become husband and wife in order to make respectable the fact that they have already become father and mother? The over-optimistic assumption that modern drugs would eliminate venereal disease has also encouraged a false sense of security, yet venereal diseases reach epidemic proportions in thirty major American cities, today.

Social implications of promiscuity involve much more than the consequence of infection or conception, for sex is a public transaction, which enters into community with larger forms of human association. Reports from Sweden, a country which has prided itself on removal of moral restraints, indicate that the human toll resulting from promiscuity has been great. And a significant movement to arrest the trend toward complete sexual license has been launched by a Swedish medical organization. Perhaps the warnings of Pitirim Alexandrovitch Sorokin, considered overly pessimistic by many, ought to be examined more seriously. Harvard Sociologist Sorokin warns that our culture is losing moral fiber and accepting purely sensate values and that, as these in turn disintegrate, the basic structure of our society will fall apart. It is significant that Sorokin is a native of Russia and has firsthand knowledge of that culture's free love experiments, which followed the Bolshevik Revolution. The consequences of free love and easy divorce were so devastating that the Russians now enforce a strict sexual code. They have learned that a society's spinal cord is weakened when the integrity of the marriage tie is jeopardized. While we ridicule Puritanism, the Russians practice it.

The being of man is not identical to the being of the animal, and, despite parallelism in biological processes, the sexuality of man is not identical with animal sexuality. If human sexuality were merely a matter of physiological function, and not expressive of man's unique nature, then the ability to perform the function would be the sole criterion, and sexual partners might be interchangeable at will—if one's partner is merely a functionary, one functionary is as good as another. The drift toward societal promiscuity, which the playboy encourages, reveals something far deeper than laxity or unbridled passion. We are confronted with a fundamental breakdown in human relationships. Eroticism, which closes in on itself, and desires a sensation and not another person, becomes a barrier to love. A contemporary cartoon, capturing the sham character of casual sex, shows two lovers, who have exhaustively imparted the best of their sensual selves to each other. Lying back, the boy says, "I thought of Sophia Loren; of whom were you thinking?"

Manipulation of persons leaves its mark upon character, and habitual treatment of persons as things may render the capacity for right relationships impossible. Shaw's joke about the rich old playboy who propositioned an attractive young woman illustrates the problem. When the playboy asked if she would spend the night with him, she answered indignantly, "No!" But she agreed to do so for 10,000 pounds; she even agreed to settle for 2,000 pounds. But when he tried to bring her down to 100, she exclaimed, "What do you think I am?" He replied, "We've already established what you are; now we're just haggling over the price." Prostitution is wrong because it degrades the prostitute, reducing her to an object to be used, not a person to be respected in her own right. From this point of view, the prostitute is more sinned against than sinning. What the playboy does not understand is that sexual union without total personal union is a second-rate substitute for the real thing.

Because sexual ethics stress the motivation that prevents the act from becoming self-indulgent exploitation of another, it is absurd to define chastity strictly in terms of whether or not an unmarried person has engaged in sexual intercourse. If the rules are to mean anything at all, they must be applied as relentlessly within marriage as without. A wife can be used as a means to gratify her husband's desire, just as a prostitute is. Unfortunately, we give so much attention to the morality of extramarital sex that we seldom raise the question of sexual morality within marriage. One of the strangest features of the playboy philosophy is that, though it says much about sex and release of sexual inhibitions, it says nothing about the home.

Sexual intercourse outside of marriage is nearly always exploitative, though, undoubtedly, there are couples who demonstrate mutual fidelity without legal sanction. Our society provides for common-law marriage; we recognize that a couple can make a genuine commitment without benefit of the usual legal arrangement. There will always be exceptional instances where two people achieve union first and then seek public or official acknowledgement of their oneness. But having said this, we must go on to say that most premarital intercourse does not result in marriage. In the vast majority of cases, when it is not previously undergirded with the commitment of marriage, sexual intercourse simply means that one person is taking from another. Usually premarital intimacy is giving of one's body without giving of one's self. Whenever two persons make use of each other's bodies, while they remain unwilling or unable to surrender their selves at the same level, it is exploitation. Often, when two people allow themselves to be swept into an illicit liaison, it is not because they love each other too much, but because they respect each other too little.

Genuine love demands that a couple preserve the final line of intimacy until the final commitment of marriage, and young people will certainly listen to this approach. On the other hand, many of them will no longer be deterred by purely pragmatic arguments for restraint based only upon fear of consequences and loss of status if anything goes wrong. What they will be influenced by, if they are to be influenced at all, is genuine moral concern for persons. We have to admit that some of the practices our society condones, such as petting or dressing in a manner calculated to incite desire, may actually be more selfish and reprehensible than intercourse between a boy and girl who are deeply in love. In this regard, the churches have been woefully inconsistent and hesitant to face realities. While we hold vigorously to the principle that sexual intercourse should be confined to married lovers, all failures to achieve the ideal are not equally reprehensible.

The tendency to separate sex from the deeper concerns of man's total being has been given a tremendous boost in recent years by the work of professional sexologists. Although the studies of Dr. Alfred Kinsey are historic contributions, as are the more recent labors of Dr. William H. Masters, their clinical mechanization of sex tends to add respectability to the notion that sex is primarily a biological function. Though these researchers provide us with valuable physiological information, they also deepen our ethical confusion.

The word "love" does not appear in the index of either of the bulky Kinsey volumes, presumably because love is admittedly difficult to measure. Both Kinsey and Masters assume that everything important to human sexuality may be artificially simulated or duplicated in the laboratory. During the monumental Masters' project, observers watched, filmed in color, and tested by elaborate gadgetry, thousands of couples —married and otherwise—engaged in intercourse. In ordinary prostitution only the females receive fees, but in this scientific experience the males were also paid. The scientific observation included masturbation as well as coition, in that hundreds of volunteer men and women were scrutinized from every angle while manipulating themselves into orgasm. This austere, clinical approach isolates the physical response and enshrines it as the meaning and measure of human experience, which is a totally materialistic premise.

Since our technological age proposes to solve all other problems by acquiring knowledge of the proper technique, use of this method as the key to sexual problems as well is the premise of the how-to sex manuals now glutting the market. The pattern for many later, and far less carefully wrought, books was the pioneering manual by Dutch gynecologist T. H. Van De Velde. In reading this respected volume, one is left with the impression that sexual success is largely a matter of proper maneuvers! All that is required to stabilize a shaky marriage is to provide the partners with erotic training so they may sharpen their capacities to function more efficiently. The feverishly sought goal of the whole enterprise is the female orgasm or, for the truly adroit, the simultaneous climax. Anything less is a reflection upon one's manhood or womanhood. Failure to achieve the physical goal, even after acquiring proper technique, may be grounds for dissolving the relationship and finding another partner potentially more compatible.

This approach nurtures the grotesque illusion that love is the equivalent of sexual pleasure—if two people learn to satisfy each other physically, they will love each other automatically. The trouble with this proposition is that most sexual problems, including frigidity and impotence, do not arise from physical or instrumental defects. For inner attitudes can make love impossible, not lack of knowledge about right techniques. Eminent British playwright and novelist J. B. Priestley discussed the inherent mystery of sex in a recent article for the *Saturday Evening Post*. "The older I get," he said, "the more I am convinced that sexual intercourse itself is far more a psychological act than a physical act, and that this—really the psychological relationship—explains the seemingly mysterious sexual successes or failures."

If one begins with this idea that sex is a mere physical function to be used for one's own private pleasure, he is led, logically, toward masturbation. According to the lessons of Dr. Master's laboratory there is only one perfect orgasm, if perfect means one wholly subject to its owner's will, wholly indifferent to human contingency or context. Dr. Leslie H. Farber, distinguished Washington psychoanalyst, has argued convincingly that if one's goal is mere orgastic relief, it may be most immediately, inexpensively, efficiently, and safely achieved by means of masturbation. "Nor should we be surprised," he warns, "if such solitary pleasure becomes the ideal by which all mutual sex is measured." Lacking the dimension of total communion, playboyism's asexual sexuality comes out a bit flat, which may explain observer's remarks about the curiously sexless atmosphere of the Playboy Clubs and topless bars.

Heterosexual promiscuity must be resisted for the same reason that homosexuality must be rejected: each is, in an essential sense, a distortion of what is true. It is the inadequate heterosexual who goes in search of the casual partner or prostitute, much as the inadequate homosexual visits the queer bar. Each is incapable of being fully human. Each practices a form of escape that differs from the other only in the manner of distortion. Social historians have pointed to this relationship, warning that sexual progression, once it becomes a frantic means of private stimulation, demands ever more intense and bizarre forms of stimulation and, left to itself, can lead to overt perversion. Our information about the past includes evidence concerning societies that started the first stage of deterioration by dissolving the sanctity of marriage and then went on to decay in the widespread practice of homosexuality. Perversion, once begun, tends to run the full course.

Just as there is a pleasure paradox, there is a sexual paradox as well. Betty Friedhan, in *The Feminine Mystique*, reports that many American women have a growing disaffection with sex, as an exhausting ordeal. One woman likened the sacrosanct simultaneous climax to a frenzied exercise in which two people struggle to reach a difficult goal, like a pair of athletes striving to break a track record. The clinical mechanization of sex and the flood of how-to manuals has given us a vision of what the perfect sex act ought to be, biased toward biology and far easier to write about than to achieve. As a result, millions of men and women depart from each embrace with a disappointed, vaguely disquieting fear that somehow they are missing the good life.

The ancient truth that real happiness eludes those who make it their main business, was never more convincingly confirmed than in the futile effort to discover fulfillment along the path of selfish sex or promiscuity. The probability is that for those who omit the context of commitment and make sex experience an idol for sensual gratification, lasting gratification will never come. Until we have reliable data to the contrary, we may infer from what we observe generally in ordinary life that sheer quantity of sexual experience does not provide the release for which people hope—clearly, it does not enrich the quality of gratification. The physical act itself decreases in quality of satisfaction to whatever extent a couple is incapable of symbolizing through it the deeper values which they hold in common. Because, as an act of self-indulgence, sexual intercourse yields diminishing returns, persons who begin by using sex purely for physical release often end by searching for new sources of titillation and for new partners, as in the game of wife trading. It thus becomes easy for people to find themselves chained to the need for variety in the source of stimulation, and less free from sexual tension.

There is a quite proper sense of inadequacy and imperfection about engaging in the ultimate intimacy without the ultimate commitment. If a man prefers to embrace a variety of partners at a secondary level, he must surrender the privilege of establishing a profound relationship with one partner at a fundamental level. No one has made this point more cogently than Dr. Karl Menninger, in *Love Against Hate*. "It is an axiom in psychiatry," he said, "that a plurality of direct sexual outlets indicates the very opposite of what it is popularly assumed to indicate. Dividing the sexual interest into several objectives diminishes the total sexual gratification, and men whose need for love drives them to the risks and efforts necessary to maintain sexual relationships with more than one woman show a deficiency rather than an excess in their masculine capacities."

We urge a larger view of sex, a view that enriches life, rather than a narrower one that diminishes it. What we must never forget is that sex is the sacred language of love, and that if one wishes to make it the means of saying "I love you," at every level of his being, he must concentrate, not dissipate, his sexual energies. We call for a more ardent sexuality and a restoration of the intensities that ennoble us. When one makes sex a plaything, he forfeits the real thing. Playboys grow old wondering why they are playing more and enjoying it less. They are missing the glory of sex because they have forgotten the sacredness of the gift.

The paradox of the playboy philosophy is that, while seeming to glorify sex, it really depreciates it. People who have a satisfactory sex life need not talk about it. The revelation of the playboy mentality is that they talk too much.

5. The Limits of Tolerance

If we cannot end our differences, at least we can help make the world safe for diversity.

John F. Kennedy

IN THE VOCABULARY of Western man, few words are more revered than "tolerance" and few have been more widely abused. The word derives from the Latin, *tolerantia,* which involves the idea of endurance. What must be endured is the fact that ideas exist contrary to our own and there are people who hold them dear. Tolerance requires endurance because it demands we be patient and understanding toward men of other faiths, classes, or cultures and free from severity in judging their actions. It demands the capacity to endure those persons and groups whose convictions clash with our own. But it follows from this that, in order to be tolerant of other men, we must first believe something ourselves. Genuine tolerance is possible only when men hold definite convictions. It is a quality available to those who, being deeply committed to the truth they hold, have something to sacrifice in granting other persons an opposing conviction.

Since tolerance is a virtue that the popular mentality assigns to the liberated free thinker, it is a favorite record in the playboy album. But tolerance can deteriorate into the weakest of all virtues, because it can easily become the equivalent of not caring. There is much talk of this virtue, but not everyone who talks about tolerance practices it—particularly the live-and-let-live group. In our drift toward the pleasure cult, much that passes for tolerance is merely a pretentious form of indifference.

From many points of view, *The Playboy Philosophy* is one of the most intolerant and dogmatic of documents. So much of it is devoted to scathing attacks upon religion that the lengthy treatise might well have been titled, *The Intolerance of Religion*. Whatever Hefner regards as evil in our present society—censorship, antisexualism, Sunday blue laws, refusal to freely distribute birth control devices to students, mistreatment of homosexuals—he sees as resulting from the repressive influence of religion. He illustrates a simplistic devil theory of history and, for him, the devil is religion. Some religious people have been strongly tempted toward intolerance, which is why preaching on this theme has won wide public sympathy. But to say that the history of religion shows a tendency toward intolerance is one thing; to assert that religion is the root of all bigotry, pride and injustice is quite another. Mr. Hefner seems not to have learned that you weaken what you exaggerate.

In whatever form it may appear, intolerance is a rather obvious sign of insecurity. The man who is most certain of himself and his truth can afford to be courteous to rival opinions. Since the chief vituperation in the playboy's arsenal against religion is unleashed upon the Puritans, we wonder whether he has ever read that classic plea for tolerance by that greatest of all Puritans, John Milton? "Though all the winds of doctrine were let loose to play upon the earth," wrote Milton in his *Areopagitica*, "so Truth be in the field, we do ingloriously, by licensing and prohibiting, to misdoubt her strength. Let her and Falsehood grapple: who ever knew Truth put to the worse in a free and open encounter?" What this Puritan knew was that any point of view, religious or otherwise, which seeks to survive by a strategy of dogmatism, or by being sheltered from the open field of ideas, is probably unworthy of survival. Religious leaders have been among the first to stress that the truth of any question is never really damaged by exposure to thorough investigation. If the faith we hold is a lie, the sooner we learn it the better. If it is the truth, it has nothing whatever to fear from the practice of tolerance.

The gospel according to playboy talks a great deal about tolerance and equality for everybody, but in practice it is perfectly clear that women are *not* equal to men. A woman is a playtime accessory, another status symbol more or less important than a multiplex stereo or an aged bottle of wine. She is depersonalized and made the object of man's leisure-time pleasure. This strange idea of tolerance goes hand in hand with the playboy's dogma of rugged individualism. Historically, whenever such an idea held sway it undergirded a system of male superiority, in which women and children were widely discriminated against and abused. Men were believed superior to women in social, political and commercial matters and, consequently, had natural rights not available to women. The woman had no recognized individuality; her social significance was entirely dependent upon men—first her father, then her husband. Because she was believed to be intellectually inferior, her career was predetermined by a system that bound her to the household, and opportunities for education were severely limited. This predicament did not exist only in the dark ages, it extended down to our very recent past. Until the third decade of the twentieth century, all females were forbidden the privilege of voting in the American democracy. Today's college senior or combat soldier who contends for the right to vote, with considerable justification we might add, may find some comfort in the reminder that a scant few years ago his grandmother was denied that right.

Under the old system, which the playboy philosophy revives, the superiority of the male was also seen as extending to his sexual nature. Throughout the nineteenth century, it was commonly accepted as fact that respectable women did not experience sexual desire or derive pleasure from intercourse. William Hammond, Surgeon General of the United States at the midpoint of the last century, wrote that "nine-tenths of the time, decent women felt not the slightest pleasure in intercourse." An eminent gynecologist during the same period warned that sexual desire in young women was "pathological." To protect the "good" women, prostitution flourished and red-light districts emerged in cities as an accepted part of the code of male individualism. In the antebellum South, the double standard was a reincarnation of the ancient Greek system condoning sexual freedom for males, provided they confined their exploits to women of the lower classes and to those of ill repute. Gallantry was shown to ladies of the aristocracy, but slaves, who had no standing in the courts, were without protection against the sexual liberties taken by white men. The millions of American Negroes whose pigmentation and facial features reveal definite Anglo-Saxon heritage suggests that such liberties were widely taken. These evils entered partially through the doorway of a doctrine of male superiority, which was intolerant of women's rights. In some respects, its modern counterpart is the playboy philosophy.

Our task, therefore, is to illuminate the need for, and the meaning of, genuine tolerance, so that it may be distinguished from this popular counterfeit. We begin with the awareness that tolerance will always be necessary in this world because men will always be different. Of course, all human beings are similar. All hurt in the same way when they are wounded, regardless of the color of their skins. All share many of the same aspirations, all hunger to be loved and long for the respect and approbation of their fellowmen. Every man's death diminishes me just as every man's fulfillment enhances the dignity of my own life. However different men may be, in some aspects of their lives these differences are only meaningful in the light of our human commonality.

But men are, nonetheless, incorrigibly different in basic distinctions of sex, race, and nationality; men are dissimilar also in geographic, political, educational, economic, and cultural orientations. Three and one-half billion people live on seven continents within one hundred and forty-seven countries, speak no less than two hundred languages, and have skins of red, yellow, black, and white with all shades in between. There are wide variations in habits of dress and diet, and drastic contrasts in standards of living and methods of labor, travel and communication. Many of these differences are of no consequence; what matters is that men disagree deeply about what they believe. Religious beliefs run from the few millions who see themselves as Roman Catholic, Protestant, or Jewish, to the many millions more who are Hindu, Moslem, Shintoist, Taoist, Buddhist, plus an increasing number who take great pride in being nothing. Politically speaking, variation in ideology is virtually endless. While Americans may be more comfortable in the presence of Democrats and Republicans, the world is also populated with Communists and Fascists. In social affairs, most men choose to live with one wife at a time, but an Arab Sheik or a Nigerian capitalist may own as many as fifty or more. The tensions that arise from such diversity are the heart of the challenge involved in living together on earth. As the earth shrinks under instant communication and travel, that diversity and its challenge become more vivid.

Differences can never be eliminated entirely; because differences that really matter arise from the cast of men's minds, not from the pigment of their skins. Intellectual divergence is inherent to the human situation everywhere, persisting through changing centuries and cultures. Although education produces changes and expands areas of agreement, it is absurd to hope that education will be the road to uniformity. Even if it were universally applied, no process of genuine education could shape mankind's mental and emotional diversity into one mass opinion. Usually, those who have attempted to establish human uniformity have sought to keep men ignorant. The human mind is potentially the most independent force on earth and, if men are encouraged to think, brothers within the same family will think differently about important matters. Probably the most dangerous experiment the Russian Communists have undertaken is mass higher education, for this makes uniformity less likely.

How shall men be enabled to live with their differences? How shall the weak be protected from the preferences of the strong? How may the consensus, which sustains a common order, be achieved? All of these questions must be asked to form any human association, be it family, religion, or nation. What is required is some unifying principle of power sufficient to transcend or control differences.

The business of unifying men reduces itself to a positive choice between two methods: *tolerance* or *totalitarianism*. One is a system of forbearance that allows for human differences. The other is a system of dogmatism, which makes no provision for diversity because it must have its own way. Wherever two or more people attempt to live together, they do so by following one or the other of these methods.

The arrangement of marriage is a good illustration, because marriage is the ultimate test of one person's ability to live with the differences of another at close range. Marriage is based upon the most essential difference in the universe—the sexual one—which divides persons into men and women. But marriage partners also differ in such things as intelligence and temperament; and every marriage manual stresses the need for adjustment, which some immature honeymooners unfortunately take to mean changing one another. Successful marriages indicate that the secret to adjustment lies not in changing one's partner, but in accepting him. Since some people like to be dominated, it is false that the only happy marriages are those based upon tolerance. What is true is that all couples who stay together at all do so either by the practice of *tolerance,* in which the partners respect one another's differences, or by the practice of *totalitarianism,* in which the stronger partner sets the policy and suppresses the individuality of the weaker.

A third kind of marriage relationship is the household of indifference, though such a marriage may hardly be considered as staying together. Often one partner takes an amused view of the other's actions and views, even in public; such couples pretend an air of tolerance, but are in truth indifferent, disinterested, and bent on their own ends without regard for understanding one another. This kind of relationship symbolizes the easy tolerance of playboyism.

Equality in freedom to be different distinguishes free society from all other forms of human association. The idea that all men are created equal is only partially true, because a democracy is rooted in the recognition that all men are created differently. Just as true liberty does not permit everybody to do as he pleases, equality does not demand that all people be identical; nor does equality require uniformity. Free society begins by acknowledging individual differences and by safeguarding each man's right to think, read, write, and worship as his conscience dictates. If, when we speak of equality, we mean this basic freedom of opportunity for all men and women, then we are free to be equal. But, if what we have in mind is a vision of regulated sameness, we are dealing with an idea of a totally different character. Free society aims at equality through diversity, and its unity is created by unity among the different.

Wherever men would choose freedom as the end, they must accept *tolerance* as the means, because tolerance is the only cement that can hold a truly free, pluralistic society together. Tolerance unifies men, because it provides them with a strategy for living with their differences.

Tolerance is an extremely difficult ideal to achieve because it makes us confront our attitude toward error, or at least toward what we believe to be error. This quality of dealing with imperfection is clearly present when the word tolerance is used as a mechanical term to describe acceptable variations in the dimensions and operations of a machine, or medically to denote the ability of an organism to function acceptably despite presence of poison or drugs. But, in our daily human relationships, we have a conflict between our own convictions and the demand to be generous to those we believe to be in error. There will always be a lively tension—and a challenge—between genuine tolerance and pursuit of truth.

It is never easy, frequently painful, to treat charitably persons who espouse convictions contrary to our own: to grant them the right to contradict, to behave differently, and to speak their own minds. Almost daily, practical situations confront us that test our loyalty to what we believe and, at the same time, obligate us to be gracious to those opposed to that belief. The instant a man is caught in this dilemma he sees that the practice of tolerance is no philosophical parlor game: it is one of life's highest challenges. In an effort to escape the dilemma of dogma versus accommodation, men may lunge from one extreme to the other. The simplest way out is to clutch one's own convictions dogmatically, at the expense of tolerance: or one may move toward a cheap tolerance, by a compromise of conviction. We must walk a very fine line, bounded on one hand by the tempting extreme of bigotry, and on the other by the easy extreme of indifference. The road of truth is narrow, with gutters on both sides.

Any totalitarian scheme, be it in religious or political form, commits the first mistake by pursuing zealously its own brand of truth and by despising all tolerance as compromise. The chief reason our forefathers were wise to separate and limit the power of religious leaders is that man, by nature, is highly fallible; and this applies to all men, including those who are in religious authority. James Madison warned that the same authority that can establish Christianity, to the exclusion of all other religions, "may establish with the same ease any particular denomination of Christians, to the exclusion of any others." Any devout believer may, at times, be tempted to wish that his faith could be named the only official one but, upon deeper reflection, he will see the superiority of a system in which he is permitted to hold his faith without fear, and is also free to convert, by persuasion and appeal to evidence, as many other men as he is able.

Unfortunately, much of religion has a particular bent for uniformity and a stubborn dislike for variety and change. Wars have been waged for the glory of God; bloody Crusades and merciless Inquisitions have been staged; the most evil and revolting passions have been unleashed in the name of truth. It has often been noted that those who are objects of persecution may themselves become the persecutors when shifts of power permit. The Christian movement came to dominate the world by adopting the methods of its enemies; and the reformers who broke the yoke of what was called the Universal Church were as little willing to permit difference of opinion as that church itself. Martin Luther himself dogmatized: "He who does not believe my doctrine is sure to be damned." Still later, as many settlers left Europe for the New World to escape religious persecution, they drifted into the very practices from which they had fled. Long before there was a curtain of iron or bamboo, men chafed under the repressive terror of an ecclesiastical one. Not until he lay on his deathbed, comfortably beyond the powers of the church, did Copernicus permit publication of his manuscript challenging the official Ptolemaic view of the universe. And Galileo was twice tried by the Inquisition: he was forced to recant and exiled to die in prison for daring to suggest that the earth revolves around the sun.

It may be fashionable to think of intolerance as the special sin of excessively religious people, but it is grossly superficial to do so. Intolerance is the special temptation of *all people who believe something deeply,* as John Stuart Mill clearly saw. In his *Essay on Freedom,* he recognized that indifference has often been mistaken for tolerance. "Yet so natural to mankind is intolerance in whatever they really care about," he wrote, "that religious freedom has hardly anywhere been practically realized except where religious indifference, which dislikes to have its peace disturbed by theological quarrels, has added its weight to the scales." Mill's use of the word "indifference" reminds us that there are two sides to every story. Some people have attempted to resolve the conflict between truth and tolerance by professing their devotion to absolute truth and dismissing tolerance as compromise, and many practicing playboys take moral relativism as a cheap way out of the predicament.

The Communists, whose ruthless methods and sense of world mission stem from the certainty that their way alone is right, illustrate that atheism can be as evangelistically fanatic as the Inquisition. It is a frightening prospect to realize that the Communists *do* believe in something deeply; that they may believe in their system more deeply than we believe in ours. Jacques Maritain has noticed with alarm the increasing numbers of people in Western Europe and America who think that non-belief in any objective truth is a primary condition required of democratic citizens in order to achieve tolerance of one another. If this idea of tolerance, which is basic to the popular philosophy, saturates our society sufficiently we will be devoured by the fierce convictions of our enemies. Our drift toward a flaccid live-and-let-live stance so impressed Nikita Khrushchev, during his 1960 visit to America, it led him to make his famous remark about waiting until we fall from the tree like overripe fruit. Our forefathers did not design a constitution based on tolerance because they believed less than the purveyors of tyranny, but because they believed a great deal more.

Genuine tolerance exists at the other end of a tension with truth and it is available only to men who hold definite convictions. It may be practiced only under situations where men hold both _deep_ and _conflicting_ convictions. If either of these two ingredients is missing, the practice of tolerance is unnecessary and impossible. Under circumstances where convictions do not clash, either because men actually agree with one another or because a monolithic system does not permit them to do otherwise, there is no need or place for tolerance. But, in a free society, if men's convictions fail to clash because they hold no really urgent ones, there can be no tolerance. It may be an achievement of some sort for the playboy to be debonair about every doctrine because he has no doctrine of his own, but it is not the achievement of tolerance. There is a vast difference between tolerance and permissiveness. Endurance is not mere indulgence. If there is nothing to be endured there is no basis for tolerance. The cheapest of all counterfeits is that sheer indifference that argues that we want everybody to believe as he pleases only because we have no settled beliefs of our own. The playboy's pseudo-tolerance easily becomes license for every evil.

Why do we so casually put up with things that repelled previous generations? Have we matured? Have we grown more sophisticated? Again, the fallacy of the indulgent playboy is strikingly similar to that committed by some overly pious moralists of the past. Some harsh moralists have failed to distinguish between sin and sinner: they have allowed their righteous indignation to transpose from the object to the subject, concluding that since sin has no right to exist neither does the man in sin. The popular philosophy does just the reverse. The playboy shifts his feelings of permissiveness from the human subject, who must be tolerated even if in error, to the error itself. Charity toward the sinner ends up condoning the sin; forbearance that thrives on a lack of interest in the difference between right and wrong comes ultimately to embrace the wrong itself. Alexander Pope's familiar quatrain, in *Essay on Man*, might well have been written for the playboy's progression toward nihilism.

> *Vice is a monster of so frightful mien,*
> *As to be hated, needs but to be seen;*
> *Yet seen too oft, familiar with her face,*
> *We first endure, then pity, then embrace.*

Tolerance may come to mean acceptance of conditions men ought to find intolerable. Forty years ago, during the prayer book controversy in the Church of England, in *Leaves From the Notebook of a Tamed Cynic*, Reinhold Niebuhr warned that the issue "ought to give us liberals who make so much of tolerance a pause. What are the limits of tolerance? Does not tolerance of a theological position which one knows or believes to be untrue become a betrayal of the truth?" Niebuhr's question suggests that tolerance may become intellectual cowardice and evasion, a weak acceptance of the world as it is. Men do not truly love justice without hating injustice, nor may they promote right by slurring over wrong. For centuries, racial injustice has found refuge under an easy tolerance that counseled gradualism and promised that, given enough time, men would stop abusing other men, naturally. We may be glad for the impatience that saw through this thin disguise and served notice that time had run out. Society cannot be tolerant when the rights of the individual are being pacified, or where freedom and human dignity are at stake.

To be a virtue, tolerance must carry the merit of intolerance on the other side of its shield. Scientists, for instance, must be tolerant of every reasonable hypothesis, but they must be relentlessly intolerant of sophistry and sham. In the human body, the white corpuscles are intolerant of germs and attack immediately when the body is invaded by infection. Tolerance of germs by the blood would be fatal. A proper intolerance involves a discriminating judgement of ideas and concepts, not a rude suppression of persons. One may, at the same time, be long-suffering with persons, but impatient with ideas. The advantage of our free society lies in its determination to find the truth by giving every idea its day in court rather than in culpable acceptance that one idea is as good as any other. Unless the search actually leads us somewhere and points toward a definite understanding of what the truth seems to be, however, free society will become a slick euphemism for a society lost in the wilderness of competing ideas, in which basic distinctions between right and wrong are glossed over. We are obligated to hear each man out, but we are not obligated to provide every nutty notion a permanent pulpit. Merely having an open mind achieves nothing for, as G. K. Chesterton once observed, the object of opening the mind, as of opening the mouth, is to close it again on something solid.

The lower one's level of conviction runs, the higher his tolerance quotient soars, for men naturally find it easier to be tolerant about matters that concern them least. Easy tolerance, because it is actually indifference, can therefore be a subtle form of superiority that reveals contempt, not respect, for persons. Edmund Burke was aware of this possibility in 1790. "We hear these new teachers continually boasting of their spirit of toleration," he said. "That those persons should tolerate all opinions, who think none to be of estimation, is a matter of small merit. Equal neglect is not impartial kindness. The species of benevolence which arises from contempt is not true charity." The cordial playboy who thinks himself noble because he does not ridicule or condemn the believer is not really being respectful. How can he be when he is absolutely indifferent to that which makes all the difference in the world to the believer? Great numbers of people, who are themselves pagan in their lives, pride themselves on being forbearing to others in matters of religion. They claim to believe in freedom of worship, only because they believe religion to be irrelevant. Belief in religious freedom becomes a high-sounding name for what is actually contempt for the religious.

Bigotry, then, may take an altogether passive stance. A man need not employ force or coercion against the ideas of another before intolerance may occur. He may simply ignore the other man and his ideas. Disdain is the highest form of bigotry. Intolerance is an attitude, not a specific action; it is an outlook toward others, and it is determined more by the spirit with which one holds and translates his principles into action, than by the merit of those principles. Formal education is no guarantee against intolerance—no one is more repulsive than the intellectual snob. And no one is more tempted toward prejudice against the lowly educated than the highly educated. A *prae judicium* is a judgment made before the evidence has been examined, and the one position a self-styled open-minded man may be incapable of viewing open-mindedly is the position he feels has been taken dogmatically by another. The one person an educated man may have no time to hear out is the man he regards as uneducated. Tolerance is the suspicion that the other fellow may be right after all. When there is no room for that possibility there is no ground for tolerance. Cordial haughtiness is not tolerance.

No more intolerant people exist than those who have recently escaped some rigid orthodoxy; they cannot contain the urge to castigate the system they have left. In *The Person Reborn,* Paul Tournier, the brilliant French psychologist, analyzed the phenomenon of overrevulsion against a religious home life. "The psychologist," he wrote, "cannot but note the personal factors which underlie their ardor. For example, their conversion is often seen to be a projection of a revolt against their background, their upbringing, their parents, and a whole mental outlook which has crushed them, and on which they are now taking revenge. Further evidence of the phenomenon of rebellion comes from a study of racial prejudice in the South made by James C. Martin and Frank R. Westie. Their "The Tolerant Personality," which appeared in *American Sociological Review* concluded that in some Southern communities, "the tolerant person may well be the deviant and a legitimate subject for analysis in terms of abnormal psychology. He may be tolerant because tolerance is deviation and deviation may be a functionally very important retaliatory mechanism in his personality organization."

These conclusions raise the question as to whether some religious and social crusaders are motivated by psychological problems. Some who make a hobby of crying out excessively against their bigoted brethren may have a psychological compulsion to cry out. So-called tolerance may become guilty of the very dogmatism it seeks to correct: The militant black extremist takes on the same aroma as the Ku Klux Klan, and anticommunism may become as totalitarian as the evil it is set to oppose. Unless the playboy is alert, he may react so sharply against the intolerance of others that he will end up manifesting the same arrogance, hypercriticism, authoritarianism, and cynicism he so much dislikes in their stance.

The hour is now sufficiently late in the world that anything short of the genuine article must be rejected for the counterfeit that it is. The pleasure-seekers are at fault, because they say too little about tolerance and because what little they do say is garbled and confuses the issue. They kindle the lamp of easy tolerance, not to bring more light, but to fill the room with smoke. Tolerance is uniquely difficult for religious people because religion is the area of life in which men affirm so much. But tolerance is not even possible for people who subscribe to the playboy philosophy of life, because it requires men to affirm so little. It is unfortunate when men lose their way, but it is unforgivable for the wanderers to set themselves up as guides of others. Playboyism promises to take us on a voyage that leads to an island of carefree utopia; what it is really doing is putting us out to sea in a sieve.

Disavowal of faith can be as fanatic as overzealous religion. Human beings have so great a need to believe in something that even those who affect the most disdainful religious skepticism tend to adhere to a belief in nonbelief; they take up the cudgel for it, and are capable of the greatest intolerance toward anyone who does not adopt the nonbelief belief. Often, even the apostles of tolerance show themselves quite intolerant toward those who refuse to accept their universal tolerance. This kind of pseudo-tolerance can turn on both violent fury and unconscious humor when an issue is raised where it *does* have convictions. *Playboy Interviews* quotes Frank Sinatra as saying: "I didn't tell my daughter whom to marry, but I'd have broken her back if she had had big eyes for a bigot." Apparently the entertainer can tolerate everything but bigots, and his remark is reminiscent of the man in Mississippi who declared: "If there are two things I can't stand, it's prejudice and niggers!"

The acid test of genuine tolerance is one's attitude toward the intolerant. As Justice Oliver Wendell Holmes made clear, in his historic decision regarding Communist propaganda, the principle of free thought and speech is the very meaning of tolerance, not only for those who agree with us but especially for those who do not. Tolerance, in a free society, means having the right to be wrong, even about tolerance. If freedom, so conceived, is an invitation to the enemy to exploit such freedom to its own extinction, that is a risk we must be prepared to take. This predicament is the condition of freedom with which we must always live. The practice of tolerance is the highest test of a free society's willingness to take itself seriously.

Freedom's strength resides in the very diversity of the free. Totalitarianism, concentrating upon the similarities among men, derives its terrible efficiency from its ability to require allegiance to one point of view. But the free society, beginning with the realistic fact of human differences, places its confidence in the individual and in open discussion of all ideas. It refuses to play favorites with any official party line and accepts those ideas that are confirmed in experience, in honorable competition with all challengers. Since it is the genius of democracy that the rights of the minorities are protected by the rule of the majority, it must always be remembered that the smallest minority is the individual. The tolerant society preserves every individual's right to be different by guaranteeing equal freedom of expression to small and great alike, to the rebel and conformist, the heretic and the orthodox. All closed systems, because of commitment to predetermined dogma, are chained to the past, but the idea of a democracy is that, if individuals are given the privilege of free expression, a better society is constantly in the making.

This freedom to think and to ask questions, to criticize and to publish is more than a courtesy to the discontented. It is the procedure by which such a society is propelled and kept on course in pursuit of truth. This faith has been central in the West since the discovery among the Greeks that reason, argument, or discussion, as classically exemplified in the Socratic dialogues, is a principal means of arriving at the truth. "The ability to raise searching questions on both sides of a subject," said Aristotle, "will make us detect more easily the truth and the error about the several points that arise."

Channels of communication must be kept open for all opinions, even the most unpopular, which is easier said than done, since our natural inclination is to deny the platform to those with whom we fundamentally disagree. When George Wallace was invited by the Yale Political Union to deliver an address, the university president intervened to withdraw the invitation, explaining that he feared the Alabama segregationist might incite New Haven Negroes. It was, of course, the wrong decision, and one of the nation's news magazines pointed out that free speech must be "for the bad guys as well as for the good guys." It is also contrary to the concept of freedom to deny any representative of any political opinion the right to speak, when he is invited. The fact that a man has nothing important to say, or that what he says appears to be dangerous, is not sufficient grounds to annul the system. Voltaire's famous statement about defending to the death the right of speech to those with whom we disagree is always worth remembering.

Intolerance has never been an effective strategy with which to discern and defeat error. From the standpoint of prudence, it is a particularly risky business, because heretics of one century have a way of becoming saints of the next. The history of intellectual freedom is strewn with wreckage of theories that were once believed infallible. Most liberating ideas have been unpopular in their own time and many of the world's honored writers, artists, and philosophers have had their works disfigured or destroyed. A host of giants and geniuses of the ages have gained the dubious honor of being censored. But intolerance boomerangs almost every time. Ban a book and it becomes a best seller; burn a heretic and create a martyr; blacklist a movie and everybody rushes to see it; forbid an idea and it gains popularity. We are shocked when good men become so zealous they become guilty of intolerance. But how can such otherwise informed people be so blind as to be guilty of ineffectiveness? Nothing is more foolish than persistence in a method, which is one of history's colossal failures.

To be deeply committed, yet genuinely tolerant, is no small task. The secret lies in remembering that the *end toward which tolerance points is always the right treatment of persons*. Since tolerance is always tested by treatment of persons, tolerance and truth need not be mutually exclusive. We may remain unqualifiedly intolerant of erroneous ideas and actions, yet be truly tolerant toward persons we believe to be in error. We may pursue truth with unflagging zeal, but never abuse another person with our ardor.

The key of genuine respect for persons insures against the easy tolerance of playboyism. It is sentimental piety to talk of respecting another person without an earnest endeavor to understand his point of view. To talk of tolerance while practicing moral relativism, smug superiority, dogmatism and bitter reaction fools no one. Tolerance lies in grasping what the other person understands as truth and judging him as a person, not by one's own standards but by his own, however misguided they may appear to be.

Tolerance and freedom are two sides of the same coin. Freedom's price is the well-known eternal vigilance, but it is also the courage Plato calls wisdom concerning dangers. Abraham Lincoln sensed this a century ago, at Gettysburg, and he raised the very real question as to whether "any nation so conceived and so dedicated, can long endure." Perhaps now, as never before, we are engaged in the testing, and the outcome is not yet clear.

6. *Alternative to Boredom*

As tho' to breathe were life. Life
piled on life
Were all too little.

Alfred, Lord Tennyson

IF THE ONLY live choice were between the playboy philosophy and boredom, any intelligent person would choose the former. But these two desperate alternatives do not exhaust the possibilities. Our analysis of the contemporary pleasure cult is incomplete if we simply point out the dangers of the present path. We must also show a better way, for true criticism is always affirmative and does not stop with mere attack. We have seen a far more exciting way of life than the playboy shows.

The half-truths this popular philosophy preaches have been widely believed, because of the incorrigible need of the human spirit to believe in something. Persons can endure great pain and suffering and privation but few can stand a sense of meaninglessness. As the Nazi movement revealed, the need for commitment is so great that men cannot long remain empty; in time they will turn to something. Hitler got his chance because of a vacuum, and the great danger of any moral vacuum is that it is an invitation to adopt unworthy values. The most frightening meaning of the fantastic success of the playboy way is that it accurately measures the emptiness of our time.

Boredom, the weariness of spirit that always follows when freedom is *mere* freedom, is one of the foremost human

110

problems of our time. Boredom is revealed by affluent white teen-agers, flocking to Florida beaches each spring vacation to celebrate a pagan festival. Boredom contributes to riots when there is a high rate of unemployment among unchallenged young men. Boredom appears in the cocktail lounges where those who do not feel needed while away the tedious hours. Boredom also contributes to the craze for travel. Some Americans fly all the way to Paris and, after a lonely bus tour of museums and monuments, spend the rest of their time meeting other Americans in bars. One of the most vivid evidences of boredom is the millions of lives frittered away staring at the thirty-ninth episode of some utterly worthless TV story. According to the most accurate estimate, the average American now spends twenty hours a week watching television. Many watch the screen selectively, but millions desperately stare blankly only as an exercise of emptiness. There is nothing wrong with television or with travel as a means of relaxation, enrichment, or diversion; but they are poor substitutes for purpose. Living loses joy when we attempt to make diversion the essence of life, instead of a part of life.

Unparalleled leisure time, a product of affluence and technology, will continue to increase so that, by the beginning of the twenty-first century, two percent of the population may be able to produce all of the goods the remainder of society can possibly consume. What shall we do with such leisure? Will man's most significant challenge be the weekend battle with crabgrass? If a person's life is already empty, the problem is compounded by the gift of more free time.

A striking example of our present duel with boredom is that one American city, which supports in large measure the entire state in which it is located, is dedicated almost exclusively to the pursuit of pleasure. Once a haven for gangsters, and now renowned for its gambling, quickie marriages and divorces, drinking bouts and sexual escapades, Las Vegas is now a favorite entertainment spot for the conventional middle class. Increasing crowds of vacationers and conventioneers make their pilgrimages to it as to the Mecca of hedonism. Airlines advertise special rates and express schedules from major cities. In some instances, passengers are promised that they can leave home after working hours and still arrive in time for a full evening—late dinner and the final floor show. To strengthen its appeal as a place for family entertainment, the city fathers have made babysitting facilities available. The biggest threat to the city's economy is the competition it is beginning to receive from every other major city. Why bother to go to Las Vegas when escape from boredom is so near at hand?

Many psychologists are convinced that it is the man or woman most lacking in self-esteem and most empty of life-purpose who, in the search for reassurance, can be most easily drawn into a promiscuous sexual liaison. The teen-ager who gropes for self-esteem through sexual experimentation and the middle-aged husband who props up his sagging ego by extramarital conquests suffer alike from a real lack of belief in themselves. This frantic attempt to buttress the ego leaves a person more deeply frustrated than ever. One simply cannot —playboy or not—derive his own value from the number of women who are his playthings. We live in a lonely crowd. If we have any compassion we are deeply moved by the sight of lonely men and women who seek to drown their loneliness in empty intimacies.

That there is no lasting solution to the ache of boredom in the pursuit of pleasure and things is the conclusion of John W. Gardner, former Secretary of Health, Education, and Welfare, in his book, *Self-Renewal*, published by Harper and Row, Inc. "It is not unduly harsh," he begins, "to say that the contemporary idea of happiness cannot possibly be taken seriously by anyone whose intellectual or moral development has progressed beyond that of a three-week-old puppy. From Aristotle to Jefferson, the men who have thought seriously about man's happiness would be startled to discover how that word is now interpreted." Later the author adds, "Despite almost universal belief to the contrary, gratification, ease, comfort, diversion in the state of having achieved all one's goals do not constitute happiness for man. The reason Americans have not trapped the bluebird of happiness, despite the most frantic efforts the world has ever seen, is that happiness as total gratification is not a state to which man can aspire. The irony is that we should have brought such unprecedented dynamism to the search for such a static condition." Comforts and the pleasure of good living will never be enough, Gardner concludes, "If they were, the large number of Americans who have been able to indulge their whims on a scale unprecedented in history would be deliriously happy. They would be telling one another of their unparalleled serenity and bliss instead of trading tranquilizer prescriptions."

Is there no alternative to boredom? Life piled on life is, indeed, all too little. Must we settle for Sartre's sad dictum that there is no escape from the human dilemma? Is there nothing better than our compulsive interest in our own little happiness? Yes, there is something better, but it is never simple. Because a man's life can never be unified merely by his own efforts or within his own consciousness, he must seek to be a new person by commitment to something beyond himself. But to what? Recently, English satirist Malcolm Muggeridge made clear to students at the University of Edinburgh how much Western civilization needs genuine moral renewal and how much he, personally, would welcome it. His remarks, published in *Another King*, pointed out how infinitely sad it is that the present moral upheaval should amount to nothing more than "a demand for Pot and Pills, for the most tenth-rate sort of escapism and self-indulgence ever known," he said. And how pathetic that when the world is waiting for a marvelous release of creativity, all we actually get is "the resort of any old, slobbering debauchee anywhere in the world at anytime—Dope and Bed."

Mr. Muggeridge puts in the plainest possible words the conviction that is also deepest in the life of any committed Christian. "So I come back to where I began," he said, "to that other King, one *Jesus;* to the Christian notion that man's efforts to make himself personally and collectively happy in earthly terms are doomed to failure. He must indeed, as Christ said, be born again, be a new man, or he's nothing. So at least I have concluded, having failed to find in past experience, present dilemmas and future expectations, any alternative proposition. As far as I am concerned, it is Christ or nothing."

I was made keenly aware of the universal appeal of Jesus during one of my conversations with Hugh Hefner in Chicago. As we talked, Mr. Hefner surprised me by saying, "If Christ were here today and had to choose between being on the staff of *Playboy* magazine or being on the staff of one of the joy-killing, pleasure-denying churches he would, of course, immediately join us." My reply was that, from what we know about Him, He would resist to the end the false notion that these two are the only possible choices. He points to a third way. A way that provides us with an opportunity to escape preoccupation with ourselves.

Every busy person has retired in the evening with his mind filled with the pressures of the day to follow. On such occasions the light is turned out with the worried resolve, "I must get to sleep quickly so that I can be rested and vital tomorrow." In actual experience, it becomes apparent that sleep is not going to come quickly; then one is unable to sleep because he worries about not sleeping. Next comes frustration, tossing and turning; and the greater the concentration on the need to sleep, the wider grow the eyes. The more sleep is pursued, the more it flees, and only when a man ceases to concentrate on the need to sleep does he awake the next morning with real renewal. The secret lies not in counting sheep, but in speaking to the Shepherd, for then a man forgets himself.

If we are to survive, as a society with any real excellence, what we must have is a new moral revolution and the person to lead it is Jesus. Our greatest difficulty is that modern man confuses Jesus with visions of stained-glass windows and high pulpits. Our necessary task is to help our contemporaries go beyond the popular caricature and to examine the claims of One who is honest enough to tell it as it is and whose ability to unify a man's life is not lessened by the intervening years.

"Gentle Jesus, meek and mild," is an absurd way to describe a Man who was listed by the authorities as a public danger. He exploded in violent anger at the sight of exploitation or smug hypocrisy, and deliberately walked to His own death despite the urgent pleas of His closest friends. Nothing is more at odds with reality than the average artists' conception of Jesus hanging on the wall of the average church library. His admirers have done almost as much to distort His reputation as His critics.

Here was a young Man, who, denied during His brief life the joys of marriage, had every hunger and hurt we have, and who knew every temptation we know. Crowds swarmed around Him constantly, women were so attracted by His charismatic charm that they sat spellbound at His feet or reached through the crowds to touch His body. This young Man, alive with intensity, drew other strong men to His side like a magnet, and transformed them with a dynamic new purpose. His alternative to boredom was of such enduring appeal that men all over the world, including all playboys, date all important events of their lives from the time of His birth. Millions have found the answer to life's riddle in His ethical idealism.

But beyond His ethical insights there was a strange, irresistible Power. This earthquake-like Power, which first moved men in rural Galilee, eventually shook the hedonistic civilization of Rome to its very foundations. By the sheer magnetism of His personality Jesus set in motion forces that transformed the lives of Hebrew tradesmen and Abyssianian slaves, of Grecian philosophers and hardened Roman soldiers.

Today, and in my own experience, I have known this same transforming Life coming full force across the centuries. Today, I have observed this strange Power at work on college campuses throughout the nation. Where formalized religion has struggled in vain to attract serious attention in the halls of academe, I have watched disturbed and despairing students come alive with a new purpose, to become involved with the hungry in Biafra and the illiterate in Brazil. I have seen the authentic pleasure that floods the lives of young men and women who have discovered something more important to do than take pot or go to bed. It is not possible to find anything more empirical than the exclamation of thousands of college students who are saying, simply and humbly, "Whereas I was blind, now I see!" Call it what you will, this man Jesus has something! When all is said and done, He holds out a third alternative that promises richer living now, and hope beyond the funeral home.

But it is not true that Jesus was interested only in life after death. His message was aimed at life after birth. Most contemporary seekers of the type attracted to the playboy philosophy have never seriously looked at the biography of Jesus. They know nothing of Him as a real person. But, if they were to confront Him directly, they would be amazed to learn that, in all the strong points of the playboy's creed, Jesus is stronger. He surpasses them on pleasure, on honesty, on tolerance and on individual dignity. Above all He surpasses them in being unconventional, for while they say the popular thing and get rich, He told the unpopular truth and was persecuted.

Here is His message about pleasure. In contrast to the popular stereotype, the fundamental note in His life was joy, not sorrow. His biographers begin the story of His work by describing a wedding party for which he provided the wine. Constantly, He had to defend himself from accusations of overly-pious enemies and to explain why He and His disciples were so happy. Though He faced persecution so bitter it reached its climax in crucifixion, His teaching is marked by abundant humor. Only those with stained-glass bifocals can fail to chuckle when they read Jesus's caricature of the falsely pious man who is careful to strain out an insect, yet swallows a camel, humps and all. On the night before His brutal death He said, "These things I have spoken to you, that my joy may be in you, and that your joy may be full" (John 15:11 RSV). He lived with such gusto and relish His enemies branded him a glutton and a winebibber, and no amount of sentimentalizing can ever confine Him to the solemn sanctuary.

Where else, except in Jesus, can we find such a magnificent example of the strength of tolerance without the accompanying weakness of permissiveness? The conventional playboy tends to be fiercely judgmental of all who disagree with him. But Jesus' concern for all men included even His murderers. "Father forgive them," he prayed "for they know not what they do." In contrast to the playboy, Jesus is the real liberal, not in the sense of being permissive but in the sense of being genuinely free. He sees freedom as a goal that can be achieved by those who are willing to pay the price, rather than as a starting point men have a right to demand. He said, "If you continue in my word, you are truly my disciples, and you will know the truth, and the truth will make you free" (John 8:31 RSV).

The great and revolutionary idea of the worth and dignity of every individual was His; an idea which, if taken seriously, transforms every social order. This concept was highlighted both in His own colorful life and in His constant emphasis upon value of one person. He was the first to make the striking statement that one person is actually of greater worth than all the world besides! He practiced what He preached by finding time for neglected individuals like the hopelessly insane man among the Gadarene swine and the despised tax collector at Jericho. In His story of the lost sheep this point is made vivid by the imprudent observation that it is right to use time to go into the wilderness to find *one*.

Though, as a Jew, He honored the Sabbath law, Jesus deliberately violated it to serve the needs of persons. When His disciples broke the religious law, by plucking and eating grain, He defended them by recalling that David had entered into the sanctuary and eaten the holy bread "when he had need and was hungry." This led to the remarkable formula, "The Sabbath was made for man and not man for the Sabbath." For Jesus, the test of validity is the effect upon persons.

In the stuffy atmosphere of Jewish legalism He gained the reputation for situational softness. One day there was an attempt to put Him on the spot, by bringing to Him a woman caught in the act of adultery, an act for which the law prescribed stoning. Jesus stooped to write something on the ground. Though it was the only thing He is ever reputed to have written, unfortunately we have no idea what it was. But we know that when He rose, He said, in effect, "Gentlemen, let's consider this situation more carefully. Let the man whose life is perfect cast the first stone at this sinful woman." As the crowd broke up to go home, Jesus did not excuse the woman casually, He confronted her with compassion and firmness: "Go, and do not sin again." He demonstrated that tenderness and toughness should be the two sides of the mature personality.

Many who have failed to take a close look at the personality of Jesus will be surprised to notice that, not only was He no legalist, He proclaimed no new codification of moral law such as the ten commandments. Rather, He set about to rescue the changeless moral law from legal abuse and to give it an entirely new spiritual dimension. He was not soft or fuzzy, and He made it clear that His intention was not to destroy the law and the prophets, but to fulfill them. He warned that His way of love demanded rather than excused. He cautioned that the new freedom He brought would place men under greater moral obligation than did legalism itself. They could take it or leave it, He explained, but if they came along they would have to go all the way.

Throughout His noblest address ran the refrain, "Ye have heard that it was said to them of old time ... but I say unto you" (Matthew 5:21, 22 asv). His tone was one of authority; His intention to reinterpret, not reject, the moral law. On such questions as killing, adultery, revenge, and treatment of enemies, He consistently warned that legal observance would no longer be enough. With the advent of the ruling law of love, men were under obligation to mean it with all their hearts. For instance, on the commandment prohibiting adultery, Jesus did not say that under certain circumstances and provided no one gets hurt it is all right. He was wise enough to know that there are more ways of being hurt than we recognize. To the playboy's temptation to use the girl as a plaything Jesus was answering, "Aren't you aware that she is a person? Do you not know that lust for or the use of another person as the object of one's own selfish intent is dehumanizing because it reduces that person to a thing?" He was telling the world that, while there is an objective moral order, it is not enough merely to avoid the technical act. Men must also observe, in their hearts, the spirit behind the law. He came into a playboy world, but He was no joiner. He reinforced the moral order and gave to it a new spiritual dimension, and the world has never really been the same. It's a playboy world—until you take a deeper look.

Jesus was much more hardheaded about life than is the conventional playboy, because He was realistic about human nature. Part of the trouble with the pleasure cult is its absence of realism. It refuses to face up honestly to the evil within the human heart. What is the good of individualism if the individual is evil?

Is it really any longer possible to delude ourselves into believing that we are getting better and better, day by day, pulling ourselves up by our own bootstraps? How chilling was that cartoon that leaped out of the editorial pages of *The Los Angeles Times* the morning after the brutal assassination of Senator Robert F. Kennedy. It pictured a dark, foreboding-looking character, hat pulled down over shaggy eyebrows, hands shoved deeply into the pockets of an overcoat with the collar turned up. Across his chest was lettered the word "Assassin," and below the ugly portrait was the arresting caption: "The world's second oldest profession." How utterly stupid to believe that the basic finite predicament has been altered an inch by those of us who continue to lust and hate and rob and slaughter one another!

The thoughtful man who stops to look at himself is not shocked at the phenomenon of Hitler because he knows that within each man is a spark of Hitlerism, waiting to be fanned into flame. The doctrine of human sinfulness, as T. S. Eliot taught so vividly, is the most sophisticated of all doctrines and the most empirical. If unchallenged and left without any sense of lift or inspiration, the human heart will tend to settle for the soft or lazy or evil thing. Jesus knew that every heart contains a seed of hope, and that in every heart is also a seed of selfishness. No man really tells the truth until he says both. Christian doctrine, whatever else it may be, is not sentimental. It lays it on the line about what we really are. Jesus provides a permanent answer to ethical naïveté.

The basic unargued assumption at the bottom of the playboy philosophy is a sentimentality about the human heart. The assumption is that, if the priests would only let him alone, every man would naturally choose the way of honor. Any ethic based upon man's instinctive capacity to do the right thing by obeying his private urges is wishful thinking, for even the noblest urges can be misleading and the best of intentions requires a point of reference above and beyond itself. How will an ethic hinged only upon each man's subjective capacity to know and to do the right thing function when men do not know the proper path? Or when they lack the will to follow it? The current fad is grossly unrealistic because of its incredibly naïve estimate of human goodness. Only the uncritical will believe that an overheated couple in the backseat of a car will be capable of determining for themselves the right ethical decision. "Surely nobody ever faced this particular situation," they can rationalize. "Nobody ever felt as we feel toward one another."

When moral direction is left to the heat of the moment, human beings are bound to fail, because they are weak. What is needed is definite ethical insight to help us decide, "No, this is wrong. We must not betray one another in this way." Why are we unable to see that, for centuries, men have struggled with the ageless tension between thirst for complete freedom and their own inability to handle it? Long ago, Aristotle raised an interesting question in answer to the Socratic suggestion that "knowledge is virtue." "Yes," replied

Artistotle, "but what of the passions?" What about the passions indeed! The sentimental approach falls short precisely because it fails to give direction to people who need it.

Jesus was no prude. If modern man is to make his decision honestly, he must understand that Jesus would not revolt at the bright lights and the mad dash, the pretty girls or the love of jest. He would not take time to debate these details. The principle thing about *The Playboy Philosophy* that would have turned Him on is the superficial idea that a man ought to live for himself. He died to oppose this premise.

What most offended Jesus' contemporaries, and what modern men find even harder to accept, is His insistence that to find life we must first lose it. "We reject any philosophy," writes Hugh Hefner, "which holds that a man must deny himself for others." The playboy cult holds that every man ought to love himself preeminently and pursue his own pleasure constantly. Nowhere is the clash between popular playboyism and the ethical realism of Jesus any sharper than over how the good life is to be achieved. Hugh Hefner tells us to get all we can, Jesus tells us to give all we can. Because the clash is total, there is no way to gloss over it. The popular philosophy teaches that to get life you must grab it; Jesus taught that to win we must surrender. The conflict is absolute and irrevocable.

Appealing as some features of the playboy philosophy undoubtedly are, they seem insipid in contrast to what is truly revolutionary. The radical character of Jesus's revolutionary proposal is nowhere better seen than in His challenge to the conventional conception of greatness and His rejection of the established goal of ambition. "The kings of the Gentiles," He said, "exercise lordship over them," thus clearly expressing the ideal of the Caesars. He proposed a genuine revolution when he challenged this value system by saying bluntly, "But not so with you; rather let the greatest among you become as the youngest, and the leader as one who serves" (Luke 22:25, 26 RSV). This revolution in values was given dramatic appeal by the acted parable of washing the feet of his students.

The pleasure devotee supposes that he is turning away from dullness and really living, but is he *really* living? Sometimes a man is living most fully when he is about to die, providing he is dying for a cause. During the last few days of his tumultuous life, Martin Luther King had a rare insight, when he said that if there is not something for which a man would immediately die, he is already dead. Those on the other side of the generation gap may not have known what Dr. King had in mind but the young people knew.

"Youth was not made for pleasure, but for heroism." This statement by French poet Paul Claudel captures the idealism and the noble vision of young people in our time. A sensitive, superbly educated generation, which has shown itself profoundly concerned with such issues as world peace, poverty, and racial justice, will not be blinded to the devastating impact the private pursuit of pleasure can have upon the shape of society. Wearied by the meaninglessness of our present civilization, many young people seek a nobler way and are rediscovering for themselves some of the ancient values.

The truly idealistic young person of our generation is rightly in revolt against much he sees in supposedly respectable society. Many of them feel that their parents are not really living, that they are merely enduring the banality of middle-class existence. The young are as fully aware of parental adultery in hotels as of teen-age fornication in parks. When they think about it, these young people will realize that the playboy philosophy, which appears—superficially—to be an alternative to middle-class boredom, is really the same thing in glittering disguise. They will see that there is the same concern for position, for possessions, the same separation from gnawing human misery. The playboy philosophy looks fine on paper, but what does it have to say about poverty and suffering? Does the playboy have any message for the hunchback? In the presence of pain and death in Viet Nam, of hunger in Nigeria, of human alienation in Watts or Harlem, the playboy world looks like never-never land. The real Achilles heel of the pleasure creed is its lack of social concern. It has nothing to say to the despair of the millions who are caught in the trap of essentially joyless work, manufacturing various status symbols and appliances, the purchase and use of which middle-class pleasure-seekers so zealously defend. It is amoral irrelevance to advise the millions of despairing people on earth to have a ball.

Weary of the materialistic treadmill, the best of our generation is not looking for a larger nameplate on the walnut door or a better grade of French provincial furniture. They are searching for a cause, a mission to which they can commit themselves and which is worthy of their lives. Not long ago, the best of this generation listened intently to President John F. Kennedy, a young multimillionaire who could have chosen the way of pleasure, but who believed that rewarding play comes only as a by-product of hard work. They listened because he was *not* a playboy. They heard him gladly that snowy day he took the oath as thirty-ninth president by saying, "We dare not forget today that we are the heirs of that first revolution. Let the word go forth from this time and place to friend and foe alike, that the torch of leadership has been passed to a new generation of Americans—born in this century, tempered by war, disciplined by a hard and bitter peace . . . ask not what your country can do for you—ask what you can do for your country."

There are encouraging signs that, while they may be entertained by it, today's young people are not buying the gospel of self-indulgence. They are more impressed by Socrates

124

drinking poison for an ideal, by Toyohiko Kagawa living in the Shinkawa slums, by Dr. Tom Dooley in the jungles of Southeast Asia, by Albert Schweitzer in Lambarene—each living life with gusto by seeking to make it richer for others. And if they search beyond the stereotype they will be impressed by Him in whose era we still live.

The validation of His Power can best be seen in the transformed lives of people who have followed him. Here was a young Man who had the courage and authority to tell the whole world, not merely that He had found the way, but that He *was* the way. His boldest claim was that He and the Father were one. "If the son therefore shall make you free," He promised, "ye shall be free indeed" (John 8:36 KJV).

Jesus did not speak with the popular phrases of the playboy or with the ambiguous holiness of the clergy. He spoke the words of life plainly, in simple stories that will never grow old. One of the great stories He told was about a father and a son—a young man who wanted to be free to do his own thing. Terribly bored with the family farm, he demanded his inheritance immediately so that he could go to the glittering city and lead his own life. But the selfish satisfactions were short-lived. Though the son surrendered himself to every pleasure, he did not find freedom; he did not find joy. Having refused to serve his father, he ended up serving pigs. When the terrible bondage of self-indulgence was complete "he came to himself." He realized that even the slaves in his father's house were much better off than he. When he found the courage to go back home, to ask for a job, his father met him saying, "It is not another slave I seek, but a son." What Jesus was saying is that every man must choose to be either a son or a slave; and that the greater freedom of sonship always involves the greater responsibility.

Is it possible that this perceptive young Leader who, so long ago, told this poignant story also knows the way for us?

Have we failed to understand that this is the parable for our time, because it is the parable of the playboy?

Those who follow the revolutionary Jesus need never doubt the direction in which He leads, for in His call there is no ambiguity. As He was entering His thirties and preparing to launch His work, He visited his home town of Nazareth and was invited to read the scriptures at the synagogue. Perhaps all wondered what text he would choose—this strange boy who had grown up in the carpenter's shop. "And when he had opened the book, he found the place where it was written, The Spirit of the Lord is upon me, because he hath annointed me to preach the gospel to the poor; he hath sent me to heal the brokenhearted, to preach deliverance to the captives, and recovering of sight to the blind, to set at liberty them that are bruised, To preach the acceptable year of the Lord. And he closed the book, and he gave it again to the minister, and sat down. And the eyes of all them that were in the synagogue were fastened on him. And he began to say unto them, This day is this scripture fulfilled in your ears" (Luke 4:17–21 kjv).

The person who follows this Leader may be criticized or even ridiculed; occasionally, he may grow weary, but he will never be bored.